Brahmaputra
and the Assam Valley

Brahmaputra
and the Assam Valley

Ranjita Biswas
Photographs by Prasanta Sarkar

NIYOGI
BOOKS

Published by

NIYOGI BOOKS

D-78, Okhla Industrial Area, Phase-I
New Delhi-110 020, INDIA
Tel: 91-11-26816301, 49327000
Fax: 91-11-26810483, 26813830
email: niyogibooks@gmail.com
website: www.niyogibooksindia.com

Text © Ranjita Biswas
Photographs © Prasanta Sarkar

Editor: Sucharita Ghosh/Niyogi Books
Design: PealiDezine

ISBN: 978-93-83098-05-7
Publication: 2013

All translations are author's except where indicated.

Printed at: Niyogi Offset Pvt. Ltd., New Delhi, India.

To my departed parents, Prafulla Kamal Das and Kiron Prova Das,
who taught me to look beyond

Contents

Luit poriar gaon
Taloke moi
Gaan bisari,
Sur bisari jaon
Luit poriar naon
Tate uthi
Bor Luitor
Sandhiya poror
Bahol bukur
Sone firingoti
Dhou nachanir
Hendoloni saon
Bor bhaal pao
Mor heroa gane shure
Luitporiar ghore ghore
Hanhi mati phure (Agarwala 2004)

(I go to the villages
on the bank of Luit
Hunting for the strain of
my song, my melody
On a boat
I sail on the wide expanse
of Bor Luit
The waves catch evening's
golden glow
And dance joyously
I look on enchanted
My lost song, my missing melody
I find them echoing happily
In the homes on the bank of
Luit.)

LUIT OF ASSAM

The Journey Begins

Jyoti Prasad Agarwala, the creative genius of Assam with the sobriquet *'Rupkonwar'*—Prince of Beauty, catches eloquently the beauty of the beloved 'Luit', a softer version of Lohit, as people of Assam like to call the mighty Brahmaputra, reflecting its sway on their life and their land.

Writer-poet Hem Barua calls Assam the land of 'the Red River and the Blue Hills'. Indeed, as the river enters India from Tibet through the north-east corner of the country before flowing into Bangladesh, it takes on the hues of red of mud and silt, while the distant blue hills look on serenely.

The narrow Assam valley, eighty to eighty-five km in breadth, has the Brahmaputra at the centre like the spine of a fish and is surrounded by hills adding to its uniqueness and beauty. Swami Vivekananda once said that, 'Next only to Kashmir, Assam is the most beautiful place in India.'

Assam with her hills and dales, the magnificent river washing the emerald valley with life-giving water made Bhupen Hazarika, the *sudha-konthi* (honey-voiced) icon of Assam, sing,

Lauhityare bohol paarok pranipaat koru
Janma lolu eyatei, eyatei zen moru.

(I bow to the Lohit's wide reaches
Born here and here alone
Let me cease to be [Acharya 2009].)

Great rivers have always been seats of great civilisations through the centuries, be it the Nile, Huang He or the Ganga. So it is also with the Brahmaputra on its 650-km journey through Assam. 'The history of Assam in general is the history of the Brahmaputra Valley plus the hills that dot and surround it,' writes scholar Birinchi Kumar Barua, reiterating that, '... In a sense it is the life giving blood of Assam as the Nile is that of Egypt; and Assam's whole history and culture are intimately connected with the Brahmaputra (B.K. Barua 1964, 5).'

The Luit is the valley's life spring

Pages 2-3: Sunset in the countryside by the Brahmaputra

For the people of the Brahmaputra valley the river is not just a great gush of water but a living entity. It is as if people cannot think of their existence without the river. It has shaped their lives and livelihood, coloured their imagination as expressed through their songs and lyrics, and has pervaded their psyche. At the same time, the river evokes a deep reverence in their minds.

Though the Brahmaputra is regarded as a 'male' river, one of the few in India, and depicted as the son of Brahma, the creator (hence 'Brahma-Putra'), people look up to the river like children to a mother who sustains them and gives them solace. True, the river's annual floods also destroy life and crops, but you can hardly hear a curse hurled against it. For it is a river that symbolises the ever-flowing life—with its happiness, sadness, love and aspirations coalescing together into one.

For centuries the Brahmaputra valley has been the playfield of many people—hill tribes and plains tribes, migrants from different lands and regions within the country—all merging into the cultural and social cauldron of the land as if their individual identities are streams pouring into a greater entity.

The Assamese society is, and has always been, an open society. The process of assimilation and fusion has always been alive and has embraced every ethnic, linguistic, cultural or religious group. ...Much was retained of each tribe, of its customs and traditions, but at the same time, much more was sacrificed. Out of this process of 'give and take' and of mutual assimilation and appreciation developed a culture known as the Assamese Culture (Doley 1980, 29-30).

The great Brahmaputra, making the valley fertile with alluvial soil, has undoubtedly played a major role in this culture of conglomeration.

The Journey

The Brahmaputra's profile is like a man's life through various phases—spending its years from childhood to adolescence in Tibet where it originates, then a full-bodied vigorous young man in the Assam valley and mellowing as it enters Bangladesh, taking on the name of Jamuna (a female name, however), and joining the other great river of India, the Ganga. They merge together to take the name Padma, until they

...people look up to the river like children to a mother who sustains them and gives them solace

meet with Meghna, another grand river, to take the new entity—Meghna. The three individuals chat together as they carry the tales of the lands they have traversed, content and rested now after the long journey from the mountains, and then they meet the ocean, the Bay of Bengal, like a person giving up on life's trajectories and accepting the inevitable peacefully.

Brahmaputra's life begins in Tibet as river Tsangpo, meaning 'purifier' in the Tibetan language, originating at 5,150 m elevation to the south of the Kailash range as Tamchok Khambas Chorton—'the river that gushes from the mouth of the horse'—from the Chemayung Dung glacier. It had been long held that the Tsangpo flowed out from Manas Sarovar, 'the lake born in the mind of God,' or Mapham Tso, 'the turquoise lake' in local language. In fact, the lake is 75 km to the west of this glacier. The river is the highest navigable one in the world at an altitude of 3,600 m for a distance of 150 km from near Lhasa, writes Jogendra Nath Sarma (Sarma 1993, 4-5).

On its journey towards the east it takes different names in different regions: Mutsung Tsangpo, Moghung Tsangpo, and then simply, Tsangpo. The Chinese maps refer to it as Yarlung Tsangpo-Brahmaputra (Sky River).

After leaving the plateau it makes a U-turn near Mount Namcha Barwa (7782 m), into the world's deepest gorge, the Yarlung Tsangpo Grand Canyon. Emerging at Arunachal Pradesh, the river later enters Assam through the Dhemaji district.

But like the mysterious river with many legends built around it, the river's profile goes on changing, according to the period of expeditions and research. For example, according to a recent report assigned to Liu Shaochuang, a researcher with the Institute of Remote Sensing Applications at the Chinese Academy of Sciences (CAS), which undertook a detailed mapping of various rivers flowing out of the Tibet region, the Tsangpo originates from the Angsi glacier, located on the northern side of the Himalayas in Burang County of Tibet, and not Chemayung Dung glacier (Krishnan 2011).

But legends nonetheless survive in oral history and beliefs. According to Tibetan mythology, a stream rises from Tise, the sacred mountain (Kailash), and it casts its water into the Mapham Tso lake (Manas Sarovar). Both Tsangpo and Manas Sarovar have been attributed with mythical qualities. 'Its sands are emeralds and its water makes anyone who drinks it as strong as a horse. This is the mythical source of the Brahmaputra, the river that flows to the east (T. and G. Baldizzone 2000, 10).'

Brahmaputra's life begins in Tibet as river Tsangpo, meaning 'purifier' in the Tibetan language …

In Hindu mythology, Kailash is the abode of Lord Siva and his consort Parvati. The mountain has two names: Kailash, the 'crystal' or Kangri Rinpoches, the 'jewel of snows'.

The *Puranas* say that the river's birth is in Mount Meru, axis of the universe. It is Asia's most sacred mountain, revered as the home of their gods by Hindus, Buddhists, Jains and Bonpos.

Even in Cambodia's Angkor Wat, where Hindu rulers had established a vast Khmer empire, Mount Meru dominates the world-famous heritage site.

The mystery of the source of the great Brahmaputra kept explorers riveted for a long time. While exploring west Tibet (1715), Ippolito Desideri, a Jesuit priest from Pistoia of northern Tuscany, heard that the two rivers, Tsangpo and Brahmaputra, were the same: 'He was the first to report that, from what he had heard, after crossing Tibet from east to west and having carved a way through the Himalayas, this great river continued across Assam until it joined up with another imposing river, the Ganges (Ibid, 15-18).'

Avian life thrives on the banks of the river

Facing page: Leaving behind the mountains

Desideri was the first European, according to scholars, to grasp the Tibetan language and write extensively on the country.

Almost seventy years later, in 1782, the first map of India, *Memoires of A Map of Hindoostan*, was compiled by Major James Rennell, Surveyor General of the East India Company, known as 'the father of Indian geography', which showed the Tsangpo and the Brahmaputra as a single waterway.

Moving in an easterly direction through some of the most inaccessible mountainous terrains of greater Himalayas, Tsangpo takes the name of Siang and then Dihang in Arunachal Pradesh at the Himalayan foothills. Downstream, it meets two other rivers originating in the Himalayas—Dibang and Lohit—and flows as the Brahmaputra into the valley of Assam. But the river also retains the names Lohit, Luit, Borluit, Burhaluit, Sriluit, etc., in local Assamese lingo. There is a reason for it. For a long time, it was thought that Lohit was the main stream of the Brahmaputra. Thus the name often replaced it.

Some scholars are of the view that the Himalayan region tends to change its contours from time to time, and particularly because the foothills lie in an active seismic zone, it has seen rivers changing courses or new land formations coming up. So who knows if in the remote past Lohit was contiguous to the Tsangpo and not Dihang as we know today? After all, geophysical evidence shows that at one time Tsangpo was flowing from east to west and not the other way round. 'Perhaps the Siang river through headward erosion gradually flowed northward and joined the Tsangpo at some point and in time completely took over the stream and brought it down southward,' writes J.N. Sarma (Sarma 1993, 9).

The belief that the Lohit, called Zayal Chu in China, was the original Brahmaputra persisted till the nineteenth century because tracing the river up to the Tibetan plateau from the north-eastern part of the country through inaccessible terrains was a great challenge. Then there were hostile tribes inhabiting the track that made exploration hazardous. Some adventurers were even killed.

The British government sent many explorers as they wanted to open trade routes to Tibet but success was limited. In 1825, Captain Philip Burlton went up the Brahmaputra by boat and found the water divided into three different directions—on the east the Lohit, to the north Dihang and Dibang. The Survey of India officials trained local talent, sometimes disguised as lamas since Tibet had forbidden foreigners to enter, to trace and authenticate the course of the Brahmaputra. Among the real-life accounts of these adventurers, which read like film scripts, stands out the name of Kinthup, a Sikkimese, an unsung hero who spent four years in Tibet since 1879. He was perhaps the first to connect the Siang with the Brahmaputra of Assam. But his supervisor, H.J. Harman, had left India by the time he returned and his feat remained buried in official reports.

A few years later, famous Swedish explorer Sven Hedin, while exploring the source of three great rivers, Indus, Sutlej and Brahmaputra, ascertained with scientific data about the source of Tsangpo in the region of Chemayung Dung glacier. He had entered the region through Ladakh. On 13 July 1907, the Swedish explorer came to what he described as one of the most important discoveries made on earth: 'It gives one sense of pride to stand beside the origin of three sources of the splendid river which pours out into the Ocean near Calcutta, the son of Brahma, that celebrated figure in the ancient history of India' (T. and G. Baldizzone 2000, 29).

However, there was a missing link between Tsangpo and the Brahmaputra. How could the river at such elevation suddenly drop down to the valley? It was only in

The belief that the Lohit, called Zayal Chu in China, was the original Brahmaputra persisted till the nineteenth century ...

'*Mahabahu*' Brahmaputra in its full glory in the Assam valley

1924 that two soldier-botanists, Frank Kingdon-Ward and Earl Cawdor, taking help of accounts of previous unfinished expeditions, could prove through maps that Tsangpo continued from Tibet to form the Dihang and entered India through great cascades and waterfalls through gorges skirting Namcha Barwa. Kingdon-Ward's father was also a celebrated botanist at Cambridge University.

One day when Frank was still young he overheard a conversation between his father and a colleague just back from the Far East. While most of it was of no interest one phrase stuck out and stayed with him: 'There are places up the Brahmaputra where no white man has ever been.'

Many myths are woven around the powerful Brahmaputra. In ancient scriptures like *Raghuvansha* by poet Kalidasa around fourth century BC and classical literature such as *Mahabharata*, the river evoked reverence and was referred as 'Lauhitya'. Later in *Kalika Purana*, a Tantric treatise written in Assam around the tenth century, and *Yoginitantra* (c. sixteenth century), the name Brahmaputra occurs for the first time, writes J.N. Sarma.

*... Parasurama
hewed a channel
from this lake
[Brahmakunda]
to bring the
water—
Brahmaputra—
to benefit people
on earth*

A symbolic story in the *Kalika Purana* assigns Brahmaputra as the son of Brahma, the creator, and Amogha, the beautiful wife of sage Santanu whose abode was in the eastern Himalayan foothills. The ascetic changed his abode from time to time living sometimes in Kailash, sometimes on top of a hill called Gandhamadana, and sometimes by the bank of a lake called Lohita. Once when he was away from home, Brahma, the creator, came to meet him but only Amogha was at home. Brahma wanted to cohabit with her and have a child who would bring happiness to the people. But chaste Amogha forbade him to touch her; so Brahma left but his passion was such that he left behind his semen. On returning, Santanu with his inner eye recognised the fiery semen as that of Brahma and his true intention. He asked his wife to swallow the semen but Amogha refused and asked Santanu to drink it and plant the seed of Brahma in her womb. Subsequently a child in the watery form of Brahma was born. Santanu placed it amidst four hills and called it Brahmakunda which expanded in size very soon. Later sage Parasurama hewed a channel from this lake to bring the water—Brahmaputra— to benefit people on earth. There is speculation about whether this lake was the Manas Sarovar in the Himalayas or the Parasuramkunda in Arunachal Pradesh in the east.

The river is the main mode of transport for many people even today

The valley of Assam has long been a land of different tribal groups many of whom had migrated from outside. They were predominantly of Austro-Asiatic and Indo-Mongoloid origins (Kiratas) and the land was often referred to as 'land of the Kiratas' in ancient scriptures. These people had their own name for the river, not the Sanskritised version. The oldest name one comes across is Lao-Tu and later, Ti-Lao (clear water), a Tibeto-Burman word. In fact, the Ahoms, who migrated from upper Burma (Myanmar) in the thirteenth century to set up a powerful dynasty in the valley, knew the river by this name.

Scholar Raj Mohan Nath has another explanation for the name of the river Lohit. China in olden days, he writes, was generally called 'Chao-Thieus' meaning 'God's Heaven Land' which was later shortened to 'Chuh-This' pronounced Zuh-This (R.M. Nath 1948, 2). A batch of Zuh-This people from their original homeland in the land of Zuh-This migrated south-westward along the course of the river rising from the hills on the south-western border of China and joined the Tsangpo river at the north-eastern corner of Assam. As they proceeded they found the water course in the river very wide, and they called it Lao-Tu (wide water) which later underwent transformation into Lohit. This is the land of 'Lauhitya' found in Indian records. The migration very probably took place in about 2750 BC, writes Nath.

Indeed the Brahmaputra valley has been the playfield of many races from time immemorial—Oceanic, Negritos, Alpines, Austrics and Indo-Mongoloids as well as Aryans in the later days from the greater Gangetic valley—who all contributed to shape the composite culture of Assam. The human interaction and their influences merged into a cauldron of tribal customs, Hindu rituals and tribal folklores. Many of the local customs and beliefs were later Sanskritised under increasing Brahminic influence. 'While there had been migration of hordes of Aryan settlers at different times, the indigenous population had also been under influence of Aryan religio-cultural mores and modes, giving rise in the process to a very interesting synthesis of Aryan and indigenous strains' (Datta, Sarma and Das 1994, 3).

So is the case with the great Brahmaputra too—its image, its mysteries, the reverence it evokes, as also a deep attachment and love, reflect many concepts and interpretations, you discover, as you take a journey along the banks of the river in the Assam valley. •

PARASURAMKUNDA
TO THE VALLEY
On a Holy Trail

Pages 14-15: The Lohit breaks through the hills

Even on a wintry dry day with monsoon's ferocious downpour over, the sound of water gurgling forcefully in the distance cannot escape the traveller's ear here at Parasuramkunda, the legendary *tirth-sthan* or pilgrimage centre in the Lohit district of Arunachal Pradesh. From this *kunda*, a deep whirlpool, the Lohit river flows down to the valley of Assam. In the distance, the peaks of the Mishmi hills look like a bedspread with an *Ikkat* design in blue. Lohit's source is at a peak called Yoko in China. It enters India at Rima in the north east of Arunachal Pradesh. Parasuramkunda or Brahmakunda is at a distance of 120 km from this spot.

Cartographers, modern travellers and explorers may establish that actually the Siang-Dihang is the main stream of the mighty Brahmaputra, that the meeting of the streams Lohit, Dihang and Dibang further down at Kobo effectively creates the river Brahmaputra, but for the common people, even for the local tribes, Lohit 'is' the Brahmaputra. Indeed, as historian Suryya Kumar Bhuyan says, 'In a sense, the civilisation of Assam can be called Lauhitya civilisation (Bhuyan 1965, 4).'

'What do you call this river?' you ask a local Mishmi boy as he walks by.

'Brahmaputra, of course!' he replies promptly.

Such is the belief embedded in people's religio-cultural memory that the reputation of the river Lohit still evokes awe and reverence.

Interestingly, Raj Mohan Nath writes of the Assam valley being compared to a woman's body with defined body parts while the Brahmaputra forms the back bone: the north-eastern part from Sadiya to Bharali in the Sonitpur district as the crown (*sumeru*); Sadiya to Dibrugarh is also called the head (*mastak*); Bharali to Rupasi river in the Nagaon district as the neck and breast (*ratna-pitha*); Guwahati to Manas river as the waist or genital organ (*kama*) and so *kama-pitha*; and western Assam representing the feet of the mother named *bhadra-pitha* or the venerated region (R.M. Nath 1948, 3-4).

Parasuramkunda is an enchanting spot. Peering from the bridge over the Lohit below, you see the deep green water with fringes of white foams crushing against the craggy stone mounds in the middle of the river. The awe-inspiring rapids merge, meet around the rocks and create a steady, deep gurgling sound. At one place, a stone island of sorts stands between the streams. It is said that the devastating earthquake of 1950 in Assam with a magnitude of 8.6 on the Richter scale, which even changed the course of the Brahmaputra's tributary, Subansiri, shattered the rocks which almost ringed the *kunda* once.

Interestingly, Raj Mohan Nath writes of the Assam valley being compared to a woman's body with defined body parts ...

Jogendra Nath Sarma in his book quotes administrator Laksheswar Sarma from his travelogue, *Mishimi Paharar Rongshinga* (The echoes of Mishmi Hills), about Parasuramkunda thus:

5 December, 1948: To the north of the Lohit river the tall peaks of the Mishmi hills seem to touch the sky. From here, like a chador in blue, the river Lohit makes an appearance. The Brahmakunda is surrounded by rocks on three sides. The water in the kunda is calm and serene; sunlight does not penetrate here. The water is very cold. While taking a dip in the water the earth seems to slip from beneath your feet - so slippery it is. To facilitate the pilgrims an iron chain to hold on runs down to the kunda. ...there are lots of fishes here but nobody catches them. After the bath the wet clothes are traditionally given to the Mishmis.

After two years he writes:

25 December, 1950: Before the earthquake the Lohit was a serene river. Now it has become wild....Arriving at the site I saw the effect of the earthquake. The river had divided into four rivulets from a place a little upstream. The third one is the main stream. The fourth stream has completely overrun the kunda. At a point a little upstream, Lohit's water crashes into the huge stones and then with great force enters the kunda. The famed kunda with so many legends around it has disappeared into the womb of the great tumult created by the water (Sarma 1993, 22-23).

Though the original *kunda* is no more, the legend of Parasurama lives on, as also its reputation as a pilgrimage centre, concedes Sarma. These legends firmly assert that the Brahmaputra originates in the *kunda* in its avatar as Lohit.

The veneration for the *kunda* is associated with sage Parasurama. On this quiet day, the place looks deserted and lonely. A few sadhus and *pujaris* or worshippers sit around idly looking at a few visitors. The steps down to the *kunda* seem to go on and on. Both sides have railings to hold on for safety. At certain points some devotees have built cement benches for the tired to rest. The more you go down the steps, the more thunderous the sound of the water becomes. At the shaded holy spot, the dark green water with speckles of white speak of eternity. Climbing up the stairs is an uphill task,

Though the original kunda is no more, the legend of Parasurama lives on, as also its reputation as a pilgrimage centre ...

literally. How many steps are there, you ask. The sadhus are not sure and consult each other. 'Three sixty-five'—one of them arrives at the magic figure as if assigning a day each of the year to each step. Since you did not count the number of steps while climbing down, it is better to accept the figure as correct.

However, let winter come and around Maker-Samkranti (13–14 January) the place gets crowded with pilgrims from all corners of the country. The dust rises from the rough roads full of pebbles while rosy-cheeked Mishmi children peep from behind orange trees in wonder.

To have a bath in the ice-cold water of the *kunda* on the Maker-Samkranti day is supposed to wash away the sins of mortal life.

The holy water of the *kunda* attracts pilgrims from all over

'Washing away the sins' is linked to Parasurama who had committed the heinous crime of matricide. As the story goes, his father Jamadagni, the sage, was known for his fiery temper. His wife Renuka had five sons, the youngest being Parasurama. One day, as Renuka went to the riverside by the Ganga, she became enamoured of the sight of the handsome prince Chitratha who was enjoying himself in the company of his friends. Jamadagni with his inner eye could understand why his wife was getting late and in a rage ordered his sons to behead her for this act of aberration. None of the elder brothers of Parasurama agreed to this terrible crime but he being the obedient son, despite knowing the consequences, severed his mother's head. As a punishment for this sin, the axe stuck to his hand. In this state he travelled all over the country, visiting all the *tirths* to pay penance and get rid of the axe, but in vain. At last he arrived at the site of the Brahmakunda and when he bathed there the axe finally slid down to the water. The river turned red with blood (*lohit*). This miracle convinced him that it was sacred water and he decided to cut a channel from the *kunda* to make the water flow down to the plains, fertilise the land and benefit the people. From then on, the legend of the Lohit aka Brahmaputra and Parasuramkunda grew and today, even many centuries later, the beliefs continue.

However, *Puranic* interpretations of the river emerging from a lake sometimes get confusing because the Brahmakunda as understood by another account, is not here but in Tibet and the place known as Brahmakunda today was known as Lohit sagar or the lake of Lohit in days of yore.

Besides the mythical attribution of the 'red' colour to the Lohit, there is another explanation for the nomenclature. The huge river, particularly during the monsoon, carries so much silt and red earth on its journey to lower Assam that the water looks red and hence could lend it this name.

About eighty km from Parasuramkunda on the border between Assam and Arunachal Pradesh lies Sadiya. In Assamese there is a riddle rhymed thus:

Sadialoy nazaba, sotphul nekhaba
kechpaptot nakhaba lon
Ratipuai ronga hoi kun?

(Don't go to Sadiya, don't feast on the Sot flower
Don't wrap salt in a wet leave
Who becomes red first thing in the morning?)

The answer is, of course, the sun.

Though a folk riddle, it indicates that at one time people of the region thought that Sadiya was the eastern-most part of the land and the sun rises there first. Today, the eastern-most point in India is recognised as Dong in Arunachal Pradesh. At the turn of the millennium, when every nation in the world celebrated the first sunrise in the country, this is where people congregated to usher in the next millennium in India.

Incidentally, Sadiya is also the birthplace of Dadasaheb Phalke awardee Bhupen Hazarika (1926–2011). He spent some years in Dhubri (from where the river enters Bangladesh) and his schooling years were in Tezpur—all places on the bank of the Brahmaputra. Perhaps the magnificent river in varied moods in different seasons had seeped into his psyche and left a deep impact as evident in many of his lyrics centring on the Brahmaputra, be it the optimistic song:

Jilikabo Luitere Paar
Andharor bheta bhangi
Pragjyotishot boi
Jeuti Nijarare dhar

(The banks of the Luit will brighten
Breaking the barrier of darkness
In Pragjyotish flows
The fountain of light [Acharya 1993, 11].)

Or, his humanistic song, questioning, like a child to his father, why 'Burha Luit' (old man Luit) is keeping silent after witnessing so many atrocities in the world around:

Bistiorna parare
Asonkhyo janore

Pundits say that Kechaikhati, the blood-drinking deity, was a tribal goddess whose name was later Sanskritised into 'Tamreswari'.

Hahakar suniow
Nishobde nirobe burha Luit tumi
Burha Luit boa kiyo? (D.K. Dutta 1981, 53)

(On your wide bank
Where live countless men
Hearing their heart-rending cry
Why do you keep silent, O old Luit
O Luit old of years, you keep on flowing?)

Contemplating
a new journey

At one time the area around Sadiya on the bank of the Kundil river, a tributary of the Lohit, was the centre of the powerful Chutia kings who ruled from the seventh century onwards to the thirteenth century before the Ahoms arrived from upper Burma via a pass on the Patkai range. The Chutias were from the Bodo clan of Indo-Mongoloid stock and were an agrarian community. They were Sakti worshippers. The famous Tamreswari temple, so called because of its copper or *taam* roof was devoted to Goddess Kechaikhati who was the ruling deity of the kingdom. Pundits say that Kechaikhati, the blood-drinking deity, was a tribal goddess whose name was later Sanskritised into 'Tamreswari'. There was a time when, 'The temple was famous for human sacrifice' (Bordoloi 1986, 219-220). The ritual was conducted by appointed priests who were known as *deuris*. In the census of 1901 the *deuris* mentioned their ancient habitation to be on the river Kundil to the east of Sadiya. The ritualistic custom of human sacrifice continued till Ahom king, Gaurinath Singha, put a stop to it in the eighteenth century though the Chutias objected to it. But they did not have a choice since by then their kingdom had been annexed by the Ahoms.

William Barclay Brown mentioned in *An Outline Grammar of the Deori Chutiya Language Spoken in Upper Assam* (1895) that the people used to live on the other side of Sadiya about a century before they settled down at the present location (Ibid, 217).

About the Chutias, R.M. Nath says that a branch of the Bodos lived on the bank of the Swat lake to the east of Manas Sarovar. They migrated southwards along the course of river Subansiri and settled down at the juncture of the Lohit and Subansiri around the seventh century. From Swat–Swatia the word 'Chutia' (Sutia) emerged.

The name Kundil could ring a bell for those familiar with Indian mythology. Rukmini, Krishna's consort, was the daughter of Bhismaka, king of the Vidarva kingdom. His capital was Kundil Nagar. Rukmini prayed to Goddess Durga (or was it Kechaikhati, the local Sakti goddess?), wrote Sankardeva, the Vaishnavite guru in his play *Rukminiharan Kavya*, before eloping with Krishna, which created a conflict with her father because he had already arranged her marriage with another king.

Around Sadiya there used to be a bazaar where the tribesmen from the hills such as the Mishmis, Abors and Khamtis brought ivory, deer musk, rubber, wax, etc., and bartered them for salt, metal goods and cotton clothes which were not available in the hills. Sadiya also lay on an ancient silk route to China. Some other accounts say that the Brahmaputra was also the route through which Roman merchants undertook commercial activities with the Chinese.

During British colonial days, Sadiya was the extreme North-East Frontier station of the administration. The Assam-Bengal Railways had a station on the opposite bank.

The Assam Railway and Trading Company laid the sixty-five km-long metre-gauge line between Dibrugarh and Makum collieries near Margherita in 1881 for transporting tea and coal from the region to other places through the Brahmaputra waterway.

The hills keep vigil over Lohit's journey to the valley

Dibrugarh

Moving south-east along the river you arrive at Dibrugarh town amidst the tea country. The river here is so wide that during the rainy season it is difficult to see the other bank and gets compared to a sea. Indeed, Brahmaputra is one of the widest rivers in the world, eight to nine km in expanse. As J.N. Sarma points out, if compared to the landmass around a river, the Brahmaputra would rank at number twenty in the world but if the amount of water carried by a waterway is measured, then it is just behind the Amazon and the Congo (Sarma 1993, 13). Indeed, as Hem Barua writes, the Brahmaputra '... never creeps, as hill pythons do, and which most rivers that flow through low-lying plains generally do, in sluggish ways. This river rushes and rushes in torrents' (H. Barua 1954, 6).

When you look down through the window during a flight, the river looks like a woman's thick hair fashioned into a braid as its numerous tributaries—fifty-seven from the north and thirty-three from the south—and their offshoots flow into it. It is rightly called a braided river. The other distinguishing feature of the river is many of its *sutis* or river branches, which are not tributaries as such but streams, that meander off to take the load off the excess water and again join the main river. Near Dibrugarh, for example, is the Buri Suti. The Kherkotia Suti near Jorhat, Kolong Suti near Nagaon, are other examples.

Erosion is a constant feature of the Brahmaputra as its course goes on changing. In fact, half of the old town of Dibrugarh is now in the womb of the river. Though it is a *nad* (male river), it has the mind of a woman, old timers say, that is, it does not let others know what goes on inside the mind and is often unpredictable. That might be a colloquial way of putting it, but basically the nature of the river is such that this change is inevitable. Even the sand banks that are formed, locals call them *chaporis* or *chars*, go on changing their positions. There are supposed to be more than four thousand *chars* on the river of which about half the number have come to be permanent villages. The 1897 earthquake seriously disturbed the topography of lower Assam, while the 1950 one affected upper Assam in a devastating way, experts point out. In the aftermath, the Dibru river merged with the Brahmaputra. There used to be a small fort on the bank of the Dibru that the British had built to repel invasion of the Abor tribe from the north. All were gone. The earthquake also raised its riverbed by about three metres. Besides, the huge amount of silt and sand carried by the Brahmaputra gets deposited constantly and adds to its shallow riverbed. The stone 'spurs' built from 1954 as embankment all along the river in Dibrugarh has saved the town but the newer part has now shifted southwards.

The undulating landscape, the salubrious climate all add to the reputation of the hinterland of Dibrugarh as having some of the best tea plantations or gardens in the world. Nearby Chabua (Chabuwa of old), which has a sizeable Indian Air Force base today, is said to be the first tea garden started in 1835 by the British in this part of the country (cha is tea; *buwa* is planting in local language). Julie Christie, the famous Hollywood star of yesteryear (who can forget her as 'Lara' in *Dr Zhivago*?) was born in a tea garden near Chabua. However, the Cinnamora garden near Jorhat in upper Assam also claims to be the first tea plantation in Assam.

There are supposed to be more than four thousand chars on the river of which about half the number have come to be permanent villages

There was a time when steamers from Calcutta (now Kolkata), then capital of British India, used to come up to Dibrugarh to carry tea chests via Goalundo, now in Bangladesh, and to be loaded into ships sailing from the Calcutta port on the way to England. The 1950 earthquake changed that too as landing at Dibrugarh became unsafe.

It was almost by accident that the indigenous tea bush was found in upper Assam.

The disruption in supply of tea during the Opium Wars (1839–1860) between China and Britain made the latter desperately look for an alternative area to grow tea. By that time tea drinking had moved from the fashionable set to the wider proletariat in Britain and even to some parts of Europe.

The first European to come across the indigenous Assam tea plant was Robert Bruce, a Scottish trader and one-time employee of the East India Company. On one of his trips to Jorhat in 1823, his friend Moniram 'Dewan' Dutta Barua, who was to become the first Assamese tea planter (later accused of conspiring against the British and hanged), introduced him to Beesa Gam, chief of a friendly Singpho tribe. Drinking tea brewed from wild tea plants and sometimes mixed with indigenous butter was common among tribes. Bruce was intrigued by the smell of tea in the drink though it was not the same as the 'orthodox' Chinese tea he was used to. Before he could collect the seeds from Gam and have it investigated properly, he died in 1824.

By the way, at the London Olympics, 2012, on display was Singpho organic tea, courtesy the Tea Board of India. Young Singpho entrepreneurs have taken to cultivating this variety with their age-old expertise.

Robert's brother, Charles Alexander Bruce, an adventurer and entrepreneur, was privy to his brother's knowledge. Meanwhile in 1824 the Burmese War had broken out in Assam. One of the disgruntled chiefs under the weakened Ahom rule had helped the Burmese enter. The atrocities unleashed by the Burmese, locally known as Maans, on the general populace, is still recalled with horror in Assamese folklore. The British were yet to get a foothold in Assam till now though by then they had firmly ensconced themselves in most of the country's regions. They now had an opportunity to intervene when one of the officers of the Ahom court invited them to help get rid of the Maans. They defeated the Burmese and the Yandaboo Pact (1826) made the Burmese leave Assam and helped the British to step in.

The atrocities unleashed by the Burmese, locally known as Maans, on the general populace, is still recalled with horror in Assamese folklore

Charles Bruce had volunteered his services to the British army in this skirmish. He sailed up the Brahmaputra on a gunboat, *H. M. Diana*, to upper Assam and through the good offices of the Dewan collected tea seeds and tea plants. Out of the consignment some were planted in Gauhati (now Guwahati) and the rest were sent to the Botanical Garden in Calcutta for verification of the species.

But it took years for the British to accept that Assam's species was a tea 'proper' because of their preoccupation with the Chinese variety. Even the botanists were at first puzzled by a species of tea which was unfamiliar to them. Prolonged research at the Botanical Garden, combined with the official and scientific community's obduracy meant a long period of waiting before being accepted that the Assam variety growing wild in the Brahmaputra valley was indeed a genuine tea bush but of a different category. Naming it *Camellia assamica* stamped the recognition of the land 'Assam' on this tea species. The rest, as the cliché goes, is history.

The British colonialists flocked to the Brahmaputra valley and opened up the jungles to start plantations to cater to the ever-growing European demand for 'the drink of the soul'. Thousands of miles from the English shore these men and women built a world of their own in the valley though it was not all that idyllic a situation with deadly malaria, tropical diseases and natural hazards to which many a 'griffin' (new arrival) succumbed. The sahibs, by the way, had to pass an examination in Assamese language to qualify for the superintendent's job.

Steamer services on the Brahmaputra between Gauhati and Calcutta were launched in 1848 which were extended to Dibrugarh later. It took almost six weeks to complete the journey. It was an educative experience for the new arrivals, to say the least. The steamer stopped frequently at the ghats for allowing the sahibs to shoot birds for lunch or dinner. On arrival, however, it was back to the basics with boxes comprising most of the furniture in bamboo-and-grass huts. They usually kept a log fire going through the night to keep wild beasts at bay.

As you undertake this long journey by the bank of the great river, it is fascinating to discover how other facets of the life and culture of the Brahmaputra valley have

Autumn has an 'orange' glow in the Mishmi hills

Facing page: The hills are left behind as the Lohit enters the valley

become interwoven with 'garden-life' culture making tea something more than just a commodity for the people of the land. Words like *palong-cha* (bed-tea), *hazira* (shift) from *chota-hazira* (breakfast), which took place after the first round in the garden, have become a part of the colloquial language. At one time 'garden-time' was set one hour ahead of the standard time to facilitate an early start to the day.

Initially, the planters faced great difficulty in procuring labourers for the ever-expanding plantations. The local people more or less kept away from tea garden work for various reasons though at first some were willing enough to join in. To solve the problem it was decided to bring in labourers from other parts of the country. In 1859, contractors called *arkuttis* (reviled as coolie-catchers) were appointed in Calcutta by the newly formed Tea Planters Association. The labourers were sourced from the tribal belt of Bihar, Madhya Pradesh, Bengal, Orissa, etc. Women were as much in demand as the men because of their proficiency in plucking the 'two leaves and a bud' from the tea bushes. That meant the children came along too and often employed though they were underage. Poor, ignorant, illiterate, and lured with promises of a better life with a *girmit* or agreement of work assured for the next three years and a bonus, they willingly boarded the ferries singing perhaps, *'Chal Mini, asom deshe jai'* (Come Mini, let's go to the country of Asom). But they sang a different tune when they realised the truth:

Pata tola jemon temon
Kodal more tane go
Hai re hai
Phaki diya anilo Asom
Sahebe bole Asom jabe
Meje boshe cha khabe
Phaki diya anilo Asom

(Pick up the leaves anyhow
The hoe is pulling me down
Oh, poor me!
They lied and brought us to Asom
The sahib said come to Asom

Women were as much in demand as the men because of their proficiency in plucking the 'two leaves and a bud' from the tea bushes

The aura of
Parasuramkunda persists

You will have tea sitting on chair-table
They lied and brought us to Asom.)

These songs are still popular among the tea *mazdoor* or labour community in Assam, commonly referred to as Adivasis today.

When the labourers travelled up the Brahmaputra, many died in the steamers, packed like sardines, due to malaria, diarrhoea or cholera breakout; some even fell off the boats as some old accounts confirm. But a great majority survived despite the inhuman treatment by the *arkuttis* and even the planters, most of whom really did not care as long as they got the workers. The coolies, as the tea garden labourers were called then, did not have an escape route and obeyed the planters out of fear of punishment.

To be honest, not all planters could be painted with the same tar brush. Many of them objected to the cruel ways of recruitment and later, when a better, educated lot joined the plantation business, a more lenient attitude developed. In fact, an enquiry commission chaired by the ruling class led to the abolition of the *arkutti* system in 1892.

The kinder planters became, in a sense, the labourers' *mai-baap* or parents; they lent the Whites an aura of *deu* or *devta* (god). In Assam, Sunday is called *Deu-baar*, a rest day set aside by these White gods for rest (Sabbath).

The poor labourers' exploitation, hopes and sorrows form the core of many Assamese writings. Popular Assamese fiction writer Nirad Chandra Choudhury's *Chameli Memsahib* (later made into a movie), a love story about a tea garden labourer woman and a White sahib and their child, is still legendary. Their exploitation by the tea garden owners and administrators found resonance in Mulk Raj Anand's *Two Leaves and a Bud* (1937). Bina Baruah (a pseudonym) wrote the celebrated novel *Seuji Patar Kahini* (Story of the Green Leaves, 1951) on somewhat the same theme.

Today, however, the descendents of these people—Oraos, Mundas, Tantis, etc., broadly referred to as Adivasis—are an integral part of Assam's rich social landscape of human diversity. The women have taken to wearing the two-piece *mekhela-chador* dress like the Assamese women. Rituals in their original homeland like *Tushu* puja, *Karam* puja, *Garaya* puja, etc., as well as cock fights during the festivals, *Jhumur* dance to the beats of the *madal* drums, are all reminiscent of their way of living in the jungles in the west; but for generations of them Assam has become their home. They have retained their love of music and dance, adding another dimension to Assam's cultural milieu.

Many of Bhupen Hazarika's compositions carry the vibrant beat of their music, such as this song from the film *Chameli Memsahib* (1975):

Asom deshor bagichare suali
jhumur tumur nachiphuru dhemali
O, Champa nahoi mure naam—Chameli (D.K. Dutta 1981, 355).

(I am a girl from the tea garden of Assam
I roam and rejoice dancing *jhumur*
Know ye, I am not Champa, but Chameli)

The journey by the Brahmaputra from their homes has almost become an oral myth passed down through the generations as they have merged with the land.

So the Adivasi girl sings:

E baap dada ahile konoba mulukat
pise, ami bihu gabo janu

(Our fathers and brothers came here long ago
But we know how to sing your Bihu song.)

Oraos, Mundas, Tantis, etc., broadly referred to as Adivasis— are an integral part of Assam's rich social landscape of human diversity

Bihu is indeed the universally loved festival of Assam. People of all castes and creeds celebrate this spring festival which was basically an agrarian festival of the tribals. As sociologists point out, Assam's Hinduism is a compromise between pure Aryan customs and Mongoloid practices.

The term 'Bihu' is traced to the Sanskrit word *Visuvan* or *Bishuvan*, that is, equinox. R.M. Nath says, 'The term Bihu is derived from the Sanskrit word "Dvishu" meaning dividing into two which referred to the date of the solar equinox, when the day and the night were of equal duration' (R.M. Nath 1948, 7).

All the Bihus take place on a Samkranti day, which denotes the time when the sun passes from one zodiac sign to another. However, there are other opinions regarding the etymology.

There are, in fact, three Bihus: Bohag Bihu, Kati Bihu and Magh Bihu. Bohag Bihu, also called Rongali Bihu (festival of joy), is a spring festival celebrated in mid April. Kati Bihu, an autumn festival, is also called *kangali* (bare) because it is the time when the transplantation is over, the granary is empty and the first stalk of paddy makes an appearance. Hence the women light lamps in the fields to pray to Lakshmi, goddess of wealth, so that the harvest does not get spoiled. Magh Bihu or Bhogali Bihu is a harvest festival celebrated in mid January around Maker-Samkranti when the community gets together to enjoy the fruits of their hard labour.

However, Bohag Bihu holds supreme and is Assam's national festival. It also ushers in the traditional new year according to the almanac. Knowing its importance in the people's life, the Ahom kings wisely made it into a national festival.

The main features of the festival are offering puja to the gods for a prosperous new year, wearing new clothes, dancing and singing.

The first day of the Rongali Bihu is devoted to the cow, called 'Goru Bihu' when the cattle at home are given a ritual bath with ground turmeric and black gram pulses, tied with new ropes and tended with special care. The custom is said to be rooted in South East Asia. Researchers observe that in Tai language 'boi' means rituals of worship and 'hu' means cow. So the word Bihu could also have come from *boihu*—cow worship. The first Ahom king, Sukapha, on arriving in the land had offered puja to Boihu. This ritual of paying respect to the cattle, so important to farmers, could have been added to Rongali Bihu festivities.

People of all castes and creeds celebrate this spring festival which was basically an agrarian festival of the tribals

Following page: A voyage up the Brahmaputra led to the accidental discovery of tea bushes

Pages 32-33: Land of the two leaves and a bud

As is obvious, all these festivals originate in a basically agrarian society with a ritual of paying homage to and appeasing mother earth. Social anthropologists point out that in the *mekhela-chador,* which Assamese women adorn when dancing, red-coloured motifs dominate—as a symbol of menstruation or fertility. The planting of the rice saplings are done by women alone in Assam because a woman is the one who can bear a child, like mother earth who bears the crops. But they never plough as the plough is symbolic of the male phallic organ, writes Sivanath Barman (Barman 1982, 52).

During the month of *Bohag* (mid April to mid May), as spring touches the earth with many-hued flowers and new leaves, it is celebration time for humans as well. These beliefs slowly became symbolically presented in the folk songs and dances. One of the best examples of this is in the vigorous and beautiful Bihu dance performed during Rongali Bihu. Originally it was performed in the open field. The beginning of the new year also ushers in the sowing season and so to make the earth 'pregnant' with crops was the main theme of these symbolic dances, representing *piriti* or love between man and woman.

The lyrics are full of symbolism and profound similes about nature's bounty. They thus reflect a preoccupation with earth, reproduction and a good harvest but their poetic quality and imagination are undeniable.

Facing page: 'Will you buy my orange?' a young Mishmi girl

Bihu songs are also spontaneous and contemporary, taking in changes in the society and surroundings ...

As a Bihu song goes:

Namore kothiya, Ishware dishile
Brahmai soroja naam
Beya naam ulale, khemiba shodouwe
Bihure geetoke gaam

(It was God who gave the seedlings of songs
These are songs created by Brahma
Forgive me, all of you, if an unbecoming song comes out
We shall sing of Bihu.)

After all,

Seinujon Ishware piriti korile
Aamino nokorim kio? (P. Goswami 1988, 54)

(The same God made love
Why should not we?)

The constraints of so-called 'civilised' or restrictive society is loosened during this festival, which is also evident in ethnic spring festivals across the world.

Thus the man sings:

Sarai hoi parimgoi tomare beelot oi
Maach hoi parimgoi jalat.
Gham hoi parimgoi tomare sharirat
Makhi hoi parimgoi galat (Ibid, 91)

(I wish I were a bird and dropped in your lake
I wish I were a fish and got caught in your net
I wish I were perspiration and was on your person
I wish I were a fly and flew to your cheek)

And the woman teases:

Ronga nodi sukale machore bejarat
Luit-khon sukaiche kiyo?
Moi senai khinaichu tomare bejarat
Tuminu khinaicha kiyo?

(The mellow river has dried up missing the fish
But why has Luit dried up?
Darling, I have become skinny pining for you
But why have you too?)

Then again the man sings:

Tumi je lahori bajaloi nolowa
Tomar gaal dukhoni ranga
Kon-no bidhiye tomak sorojile
Bukut sumthira tenga (Ibid, 82)

(You, O darling, do not come out
Your two cheeks are red
Which God it was that created you
You have oranges on your bosom.)

The songs are accompanied by the pulsating beat of the dhol, flute, *pepa* (buffalo horn pipe), *gagana* (Jew's harp), *toka* (bamboo clapper), *sutuli* (clay-pipe), etc.

Bihu songs are also spontaneous and contemporary, taking in changes in the society and surroundings though nature remains the main theme along with its relation to man. Take, for example, this song:

Noiye gumgumai company zahaje
Dhenki gumgumai thora
Buke somsomai mon kuruliai jiyori hobore pora

(The river throbs with the sound of the Company's ferry
The rice pounding *dhenki* throbs with the beat of the pedal
My heart pounds, my mind gets restless
I am a young maiden now)

Here the 'Company's ferry' clearly refers to the river ferries going up and down the Brahmaputra during the British 'Company' days.

The Luit is omnipresent in many Bihu songs too:

Sirip sirip kori kapur dhui achilu, siri luitoloi sai
Siri luitedi kirili mariye
Senai nao mari jai

(I was washing clothes by the Sri Luit—pining
When my beloved went by singing in his boat)

Huchari singing is also a part of Bohag Bihu but its tone is more subdued with shades of religious tenor. Basically it is a community singing session but here only males take part. They form a group and visit from house to house to bless the families in the new year, which traditionally begins from the first day of the *Bohag* month. Accompanied by dhols and cymbals, they sing:

Krishnai murore Bokul phool apahi
Niyor pai mukoli hol
Oi gobindai Ram (Datta and Sarma 1994, 60)

(Being soaked in the dew
On the head of Krishna

Facing page: It's time to go home

The Bokul flower unfolds its petals
O Govinda, O Rama)

The Vaishnavite influence on these songs or vice versa, that is, the Vaishnavites taking into their fold a basically folk festival, is quite palpable in *Huchari* songs with Lord Krishna dominating the compositions.

The householders too offer the group some money, betel nuts and paan and kneel down with reverence to accept their blessings however exalted in society they may be. A *Huchari* party should never be sent away without showing the respect due to them.

In a way, with emphasis on weaving, food and social customs, the Bihu songs have preserved the essence of Assamese society and have tremendous value as folk elements in the oral tradition.

Among the tribes, the Mishings (earlier called Miris) celebrate the Bihu with equal fervour though they have their own festival of 'Ali-ai-ligang' (seed-sowing festival) too during February–March.

The Mishings occupy a significant position in the rich fabric of the Brahmaputra valley and '... offer an outstanding example of the processes of acculturation, integration and assimilation that have been consistently at work in the making of the composite Assamese culture,' writes folklore scholar Birendranath Datta (Ibid, 82). They have been living in upper Assam by the mighty Brahmaputra and its tributaries like Subansiri, Dihing, Dibang, Dhansiri, Bharali, etc., for centuries and their songs too reflect their affinity for nature and the river.

All the tribes of the North East celebrate the spring festival in their own way but free mixing between males and females, choosing one's life partner, and dancing together are some of the common themes. The Bodos call their festival 'Baisakhu' and the Rabhas 'Baikhu'. In these festivals too young men and women sing and dance with erotic overtones.

There was a time when the genteel class nurtured by Victorian mores in the colonial times considered Bihu dance and songs too vulgar to be encouraged and suggested that these should be confined to the lower echelon of society. Lakshminath Bezbarua, the foremost litterateur of Assam, educated in Calcutta and married into the Tagore family, saw to it that *Bihu Geet* (Bihu songs) was given due importance. Later Jyoti

In a way, with emphasis on weaving, food and social customs, the Bihu songs have preserved the essence of Assamese society ...

Prasad Agarwala and his artiste colleague Bishnu Rabha included Bihu songs in their repertoire of *Loka Geet* (folk songs) of Assam.

Today Bihu dance is so integrated into the cultural identity of Assam that a performance of this dance is instantly recognised as part of Assam's socio-cultural life.

Other songs close to the Assamese rural folk are *Naoriya Geet* (boatman's songs) and *Bon Geet* (woodman's songs). Of the first, John Butler observes, 'Assam is so intersected by rivers that The Assamese prefer moving about in their little canoes to travelling by land; the Dooms or Nudeals (watermen) seem greatly to enjoy themselves on these boat trips, for they are always singing songs as they paddle along' (Butler 1855, 220). In his book, *Travels and Adventures in the Province of Assam*, Butler also includes some of these songs, translated, such as:

Keep the boithas cheerly going
Rough and fierce the river's flowing
Ram bol, Hurry (sic) bol
Hurry bol aee. (Ibid)

'Hurry' obviously refers to Hari, another name of Lord Krishna.

Indeed, the river is always there in the songs of the land, sung with yearning, love, and as a symbol of eternity, in the Brahmaputra valley. ●

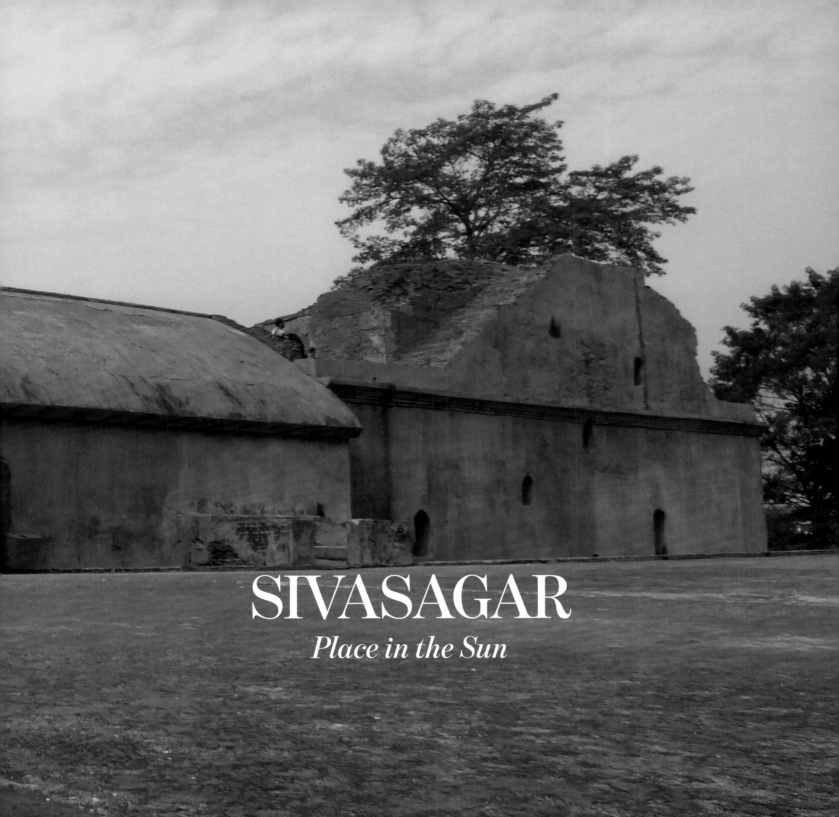

SIVASAGAR

Place in the Sun

From Dibrugarh down to Sivasagar (earlier called Sibsagar) it takes only one and a half hours by road, but it is as if another world awaits you. It is after all, the 'Ahom heritage' country. For six hundred years this race, which had come from the Shan province of Burma on the bank of the Irrawaddy via the Pangsau Pass in the Patkai range, ruled the Assam valley. Sivasagar was their seat of power. Different tribes at different periods had dominated in the Brahmaputra valley but the Ahoms' rule was the most powerful and the steadiest. Their long reign was remarkable and is regarded as the golden period in Assam's history. In fact, some pundits say that the name Assam, Asom in Assamese (peerless), echoes the nomenclature 'Ahom'. In ancient times this land was known as Pragjyotishpur (land of the eastern light) and later, as Kamarupa.

Strictly speaking, Sivasagar is not on the bank of the Brahmaputra but on its famous tributary Dikhow ('deep river' in Bodo language). The river could have once flowed through the town as the existence of a few wetlands like Mori beel and Ghuli beel in the town indicate (Sarma 1993, 45). There were also river ports around here at Nazira and was the centre of the ruling kingdom's naval power.

Incidentally, 'di' in Bodo language means 'water' and in many rivers of Assam the prefix 'di' is a common element. The Bodos had migrated before the Ahoms.

In Ahoms' time Rangpur, present-day Sivasagar, was the state capital. From there when the officials had to go to the west, to Guwahati, for example, they used the Brahmaputra and on their way, also stopped by at important points of administration to keep track of the officers and the work designated to them. Sukapha, the founder of Ahom dynasty, crossed the Patkai hills around 1228, more by accident than design, and launched his new kingdom in the Brahmaputra valley. The capital was established at Charaideo, 25 km from Sivasagar, in 1261. The capital was shifted in 1403 by a descendent. In fact, the Ahoms changed their capital seven times but Charaideo remained a revered site for them and the *maidams* or burial places for the kings in the fashion of small pyramids remained there.

The Ahoms reverentially called the Brahmaputra as Nam-Dao-Phi—'the river of the star-god'. It had a role in the Ahoms' migration pattern too as the kingdom spread progressively from east to west skirting the river. Other Shan tribes like

Sivasagar got its name from the huge man-made tank—a *'sagar'* or sea

Pages 40-41: Ruins of the Talatal Ghar speak of glorious Ahom days

Facing page: The iconic Sivadol in Sivasagar

The trident on top of the Sivadol

the Khamtis, Phakiyals, etc., followed them later to settle down in different parts of upper Assam.

Hem Barua rightly observes: '... the mountain pass across the Patkoi (sic) range has a historical significance for the country; it can easily be described as the Khyber of the east....[Ahoms] succeeded in changing the colour and complex of the country to a great extent' (H. Barua 1954, 2).

The verdant terrain of the Brahmaputra valley has an alluring quality that has enticed people from neighbouring countries to come and settle down through many centuries. Each influx brought in its trail the staple of its own culture only to be woven into the general texture of the culture of the soil. 'The abundant supply of food and the bracing climate made the people of both the plains and the hills simple, cheerful, easily contented, and indolent. These factors have further encouraged them to live a colourful open-air life throbbing with the rhythm of art, music and dance' (B.K. Barua 1964, 5).

After entering the region, the Ahoms used the river way extensively to arrive at the valley proper to establish their kingdom. By that time they had defeated, or made alliances with, the tribes who were in power in upper Assam, like the Chutias in the east and the Bodo-Kacharis in the central part. Mir Jumla, Governor of Bengal, who attacked Assam (1662–1663) was the only invader who was temporarily successful in breaking the formidable Ahom defence against outsiders as he could march upto Gargaon, the capital, accompanied by 12,000 cavalry and 30,000 infantry; but his triumph was short-lived as the crippling monsoon, diseases and guerrilla attacks by the Ahoms soon depleted his army and he had to beat a hasty retreat after signing a treaty with the Ahom king. It was among the seventeen attacks by the Mughals against the Ahoms. Mir Jumla had appointed Shihabuddin Talish, a Persian, to chronicle the Assam 'experience'. The result, *Tarikh-i-Asham,* offers glimpses of Assam during those times and says that boats were the main means of transport in the land. Around 32,000 boats were going up and down in one month itself.

'The Ahoms called themselves Tai (of celestial origin),' writes historian Edward A. Gait (Gait 1933, 78)—a name by which the Shans still designate themselves. Even today the Ahoms call themselves Tai-Ahoms.

A point worth remembering is that the Ahoms, like many Tai groups spread across South East Asia upto Vietnam, were non-Buddhists (non-Theravada), and their religious and sacred ceremonies were, and are, wherever applicable, performed by a class of priests uniformly called 'Mo' or 'Maw' in Tai languages, both in Assam and in Vietnam.

The reference to Tai or Shan race is first found in the history of Yunnan in southern China. They later migrated to upper Burma. In the sixth century they descended to the valley of Sheweli from the mountainous region.

When the Ahoms arrived, the Brahmaputra valley was effectively divided into independent kingdoms though the people more or less spoke the same language. The Ahoms, '... for the first time in Assam's history brought together the various racial groups under a common hegemony' (P. Goswami 2008, 61). Among the many accomplishments credited to the Ahoms was their *buranji* (historical chronicle). These meticulously kept diaries of their migration, beliefs and, later, court proceedings under the *swargadeo* (the king who was a god-like figure), are invaluable for compiling the history of Assam. In fact, the Ahoms were the only tribe in the North East to have a recorded history of their migration from the South East or further north. Other tribes usually depended on oral history to tell their stories.

The Ahoms were a warrior race but they were also wise enough to assimilate with the local people through marriage alliances or merging with the ambience of the land. Later they adopted the local language though for official purpose, they retained their own language affiliated to Sino-Tibetan Thai roots. Later even this native language was abandoned in preference for Assamese.

The contribution of the Ahoms to the development of Assamese cultural and social life is undeniable. Among others, they introduced wet-rice cultivation in

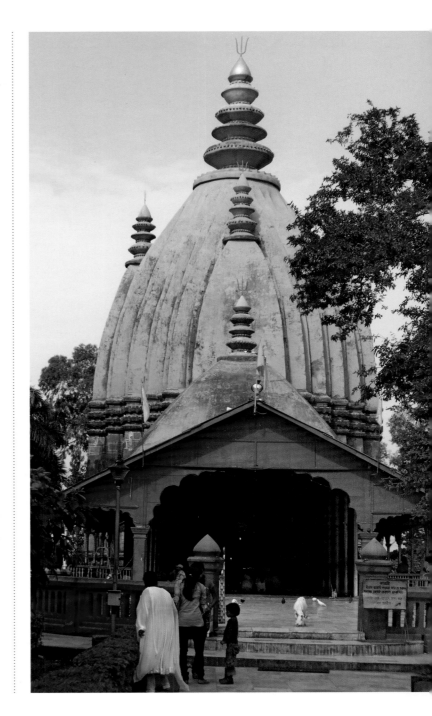

Going down history's
notebook: Talatal Ghar

the valley which was full of jungles and marshy lands. As is well-known, traditional Tai culture is intimately connected with rice-growing in low lands. Before their advent, the local tribal people cultivated *ahu* rice by slash and burn method as they were unaware of the method of transplanting paddy stocks by water management. Under the Ahoms it resulted in growth of villages around the *pathar* or paddy fields. The *bhorals* or granaries were built on stilts to avoid getting the grains wet in this high-monsoon region. These features become abundantly familiar when you travel through the Assam valley (Phukan 2008, 72).

'... Wherever the Tai people dominate, there appears to be the cultivation of glutinous (sticky) rice. The Tai people thus appear to have spread this type of rice over mainland Southeast Asia and Northeast India' (Phukon 2009).

About paddy cultivation, however, R.M. Nath says that it came to the region from China, the first homeland of paddy, even earlier, with migrant tribes from that region.

Assam is a conglomeration of two different cultural streams—Mongoloid culture from beyond the borders in the east and Sanskritised influences from the Gangetic valley in the west—and has retained the essence of both. It is reflected in the food habit of the people of the valley too. Though usually people do not consume sticky rice as staple food, the use of *bora saul*, a delicious sticky rice to be mixed with milk and jaggery, is common in Assamese villages. It is so sticky that in Ahom days it was even used for cementing structures. *Bora saul* powder is also mandatory for making *pitha*, the traditional snack during the Bihu festival.

Another variety, *kumal saul*, may not have come with the Ahoms but this rice, literally meaning soft rice, just needs to be soaked in water until soft and then can be consumed mixed with curd or milk. The remarkably proficient Ahom soldiers carried this ready-to-eat meal with them while marching to the battlefield. As per reports, researchers at Titabor Rice Research Station in upper Assam have developed a variety called *agonibora* from the existing variety, and other states with compatible agricultural lands are now trying to introduce this stock. These traditional snacks, with little or no use of oil at all, and absence of too much fried stuff, are a distinguishing feature of Assamese cuisine.

Another delicious way of cooking rice is to stuff rice grains, usually the sticky variety, with water in the hollow of a young piece of bamboo, seal with banana leaves and let it cook over simmering charcoal fire night-long; next day you break the bamboo pipe open and serve the rice with milk and jaggery. This is called *sunga-pitha*; *sunga* literally means an elongated hollow pipe.

With scarcity of salt in this land-locked region, indigenous people also improvised an ingredient called *khar* by burning dried plantain leaves in a special way and using it extensively in food preparations. In fact, the recipe *khar*, a thick curry eaten as a first course, is an integral part of traditional Assamese lunch.

Bamboo shoot is also an essential part of Assamese cuisine. Bamboo shoot, of course, is contiguous to cuisine in South East Asia as well.

Social historian Lila Gogoi chronicles how some of the agricultural species that the Ahoms brought along have now become a component of Assamese cuisine as well as materials for daily use. *Ahom-bogori* (a kind of jujube), *Ahom-sali* (*sali* variety of paddy), *Ahom-atha* (a kind of gum), *Ahom-kapur* (Ahom clothes), *Ahom-mekhela*,

... the use of bora saul, *a delicious sticky rice to be mixed with milk and jaggery, is common in Assamese villages*

nara-jangphai (kind of ornament-making material in amber colour), *baan-kahi* (tray with stand) and *maihang* (metallic plate with legs used by the nobles for dining), are some of them (Gogoi 1982, 76).

There is an interesting write-up in the *Assam Review* (May 1928), the Bible of the tea planters those days, referring to tea and the Ahoms:

> *There were tea estates in Assam before Mr Bruce's (Robert) day. He came across an area, three hundred yards square, on the Tipam Hill in Upper Assam under cultivation of tea. He also met an old Ahom who said 'It was Sooka (Sooka-pha) or the first Kacharry (Ahom) Rajah of Assam who brought the tea plant from Munkum. He said it was written in his puthi or history. If this 'Sooka' be Sukapha, the first Ahom conqueror of Assam, then the introduction of tea can be traced to the middle of the thirteenth century.*

Who knows on which page in history, or botanical history for that matter, there are hidden facts that deviate from the known history of tea in Assam? Or did the Ahoms, who ushered in many changes in Assam, have a hand in this modern avatar of the brew too—a brew now on the verge of being declared the national drink of India?

The North East is well-known for handwoven textiles. The practice of rearing silkworms and weaving by women-folk is embedded in the textile tradition of the state. Importantly, in Assam there is no special class of weavers as in many states because a loom is an integral part of an Assamese household. The weaving tradition in the valley enchanted Mahatma Gandhi when he visited Assam as he came across a loom in every home. Though these days, especially in towns and cities, weaving at home is not possible any more, handwoven clothes remain as popular as ever and thanks to the patronage, the art of weaving is very much alive in Assam. Catering to modern taste and demand, it has also branched into production of household linen, accessories, etc.

Muga silk with beautiful geometric designs on *mekhela-chador* and clothes, the warm *eri* shawls and *pat* silk trace their rapid development to the Ahoms which, pundits say, were introduced into the land by the Bodos.

During Rongali Bihu festival, it is customary for women to gift the men-folk with a *bihuan* or *gamosa* (handwoven towel with red border).

Numerous Bihu songs have lyrics with reference to weaving:

Facing page: Remains of the Day: Talatal Ghar

Thus Assam reigns as the only place in the world where the golden fabric [Muga] can be produced ...

Otikoy senehar mugare muhura
tatokoi senehar maku
Tatokoi senehar bohagor bihuti,
napati kenekoi thaku

(Dear is the *Muga* reel, dearer is the shuttle
Even dearer is the Bohag Bihu
How can I not celebrate it with joy?)

Muga still remains unique in the world of silk. 'Red as the sun, as soft as the surface of the gem, woven while the threads are very wet, and of uniform or mixed texture,' is how Kautilya, the famous economist-politician at Chandragupta Maurya's court in the Middle Ages, is said to have described the golden fabric (*Arthashastra*: book II, chapter 11, sloka 104). P.C. Choudhary says that, 'The art of sericulture –rearing cocoons-were known as early as the *Ramayana*' (Phukon 2009). In the epic's *Kiskindhya Kanda* chapter the land is referred to as '*kasakaranambhumih*' (the country of cocoon rearers).

The botanical name of *Muga* (*Antheraeaassama*) shows the worm to be indigenous to the state. Thus Assam reigns as the only place in the world where the golden fabric can be produced because the worm too needs certain environmental conditions necessary for rearing in the open as present in Assam. The tribals are experts at rearing, collecting and using lac to give that reddish sheen to the thread. Nearby Garo hills, part of Meghalaya now, produces some *Muga* silk too.

The Ahom kings prized *Muga* silk so much that common people were banned from using this fabric. Only the king, his relatives, noblemen and their families were allowed to sport apparels made with this silk. Queen Ambika, wife of Siva Singha (1714–1744), herself an expert weaver, trained women in the art of weaving in her palace.

Ahom women believed that a soldier going to the battle wearing a garment woven in a single night would return home victorious. Common soldiers could not afford and nor were they allowed to use *Muga* silk, so it could be of *eri* or any other thread such as cotton.

Though basically a warrior race, and fiercely protective about keeping at bay invasions from without, the Ahoms were also connoisseurs of art. They encouraged development of Assamese literature, arts and local crafts. Especially in the eighteenth century, under the patronage of the Ahom kings, books of various genres saw the light of day, whether they were centred on religion, lyrical dramas like *Sakuntala Kavya*, *Usha Haran*, or translations of pan-Indian literary works. The *buranjis* were originally written in the Tai language but from the seventeenth century they were written in chaste Assamese, establishing once again how the Ahoms merged with the culture of the Brahmaputra valley. Assamese language developed from the Purba Magadhi Prakrit of present-day Bihar but many tribes inhabiting the valley and the hills around spoke in the language of the Tibeto-Burman family; hence there is much intermingling in the language too.

Music did not lack patronage either under the Ahoms. Some of the Ahom kings even composed songs, like the illustrious Rudra Singha, his brother Siva Singha, and later Pramatta Singha, Rajeswar Singha, etc. The most famous king was Rudra Singha (1696–1714) who was often compared to Akbar for his liberal views and

The golden fabric of *Muga* is unique to Assam
(Photo courtesy: Pitamber Newar)

Women love the colourful geometric designs on their *mekhela-chador*

statesmanship. He even established extensive trade with Tibet. He had a pan-Indian outlook and kept in touch with developments outside the state. So he sent officers outside Assam and invited skilled craftsmen to settle down with offers of land and money. He brought pundits from the Gangetic valley and Bengal to teach children in the schools he set up. He even brought in musicians from outside and had them settle down in the land with grants of land and remuneration. The *buranji* of his reign also notes that some dancers were sent outside the state to learn the art of dancing and later they performed at the raj durbar. A group of men were sent to Delhi to learn the art of playing the *pakhwaj*, a percussion instrument. A book on the different mudras in dance movements, *Srihasta Muktabali,* was translated into Assamese during this period. Even the dress of Assamese people went through some change in his time. He wanted Assam to join the Indian mainstream and not remain isolated, albeit keeping the land's independent stance in mind, and sent special officials to learn about dresses noblemen wore in other parts of India. From his time apparels like *pag-jama* (pajama), *pag* (turban), etc., entered the fashion book of Ahom kings. However, many noblemen criticised this move of introducing clothes from the Mughal court because till the reign of Chakradhwaj Singha (1673–1690), Assamese people had never used a piece of cloth which did not belong to Assam.

Like the Assamese woven clothes, traditional Assamese jewellery is also famous for its distinctive style. The Ahom kings patronised jewellers and also donned jewellery to embellish their dresses. In fact, they made it compulsory for officials to be suitably adorned.

The Luit, as also Subansiri, literally the *Swarnanadi* or 'river of gold', were known for carrying gold particles from their source in Tibet. The Tezpur grant of *Vanamaladevarman*, as quoted by archaeologists, talks of the Lauhitya carrying gold dust from the Kailash mountain. Kautilya mentioned *suvarnakundya* or 'land of gold' to be located in Kamarupa. During the Ahom rule, there was a particular class of people with the title of *sonowals* who were assigned with the task of extracting gold from these rivers. They had to pay a certain amount of money or contribute part of the extracted gold to the royal coffer.

The *sonowals* were experts at collecting gold particles by observing the river's behaviour. When the river was in spate, due to erosion, on the opposite side a *char* formed. They would examine the sand and if gold dust was found they would block the stream. Later they would mix the collected dust with mercury, filled into snail crust and steamed over *nahar* wood fire; when the mercury disappeared and the crusts burned into *choon* or lime, solid gold appeared. It was then dipped into water to check the purity. If the gold nugget sank it was considered to be of good quality. More than 20,000 *sonowals* were engaged in this gold mining, locally called *son-komowa*. During the reign of Chakradhwaj Singha, according to reports, the royal coffer held 5000 *tola* of gold. The pristine quality of gold from this region was famous. Traditional Assamese jewellery uses *paat-son* or 24 carat gold leaf.

There was a clear distinction between jewellery for men and those for women. The men also wore chains with pendants and noblemen even wore *gam-kharu*, a large bracelet made of silver or gold and held together with a clasp. There were whole villages called *sonarigaon* (village of jewellers) which produced beautiful ornaments. Today only in pockets near Jorhat town and Nagaon are there families who turn out these traditional designs.

There were whole villages called sonarigaon (village of jewellers) which produced beautiful ornaments

As gold was available locally through 'gold-washing', the metal was used abundantly, often in 24 carat, and then combined with stones and beads which also show the influence of tribes who sport multicoloured beads. The Mughal influence later introduced *minakari* or enamelling work. Rubies from Burma, considered the best in the world, and emeralds too from the region, were widely used for embellishment. Interestingly, unlike in other regions, the jewellers of typical Assamese jewellery do not mix copper with gold but silver. Besides, they can be worn on both sides. Most of the Assamese jewellery are hollow inside, filled with lac, and the outer parts are wrapped with *pat-son*, thin leaves of gold. Jugal Das in his book *Gohona-Gathori* (Jewelleries) writes that this particular style associated with Assam evolved only after the Ahoms came and combined different influences, even from countries like Burma and Thailand (Das 1988, 31). Older accounts of Assam (Pragjyotishpur) show prevalence of pan-Indian designs in the jewellery.

The traditional ornaments of Assam include earrings like *kerumoni*, *thuriya* (flower motifs), *loka- paro*, bangles and bracelets like *gam-kharu*, *muthi-kharu*, and necklaces like *doog-doogi*, *jonbiri*, *dholbiri* (drum pendant), *bena* (crescent-shaped pendant), *gal-pata* (choker), to name a few. *Loka-paro*, a favourite with Ahom kings, is an earring embellished with twin pigeons (*paro*), placed back to back. This may be in gold, ruby, *minakari* work, or even in plain enamel coating.

In contrast to these ornaments from upper Assam, in lower Assam, centred around Barpeta, are filigreed ornaments (*rewai*) without stone setting or *minakari* work. In this style gold wires are turned and twisted into beautiful shapes of which *sona* earrings are most famous.

The Ahoms were into construction in a big way too—building numerous temples— some new, some constructed over ruined older ones. They built ramparts, roads and also dug large ponds for common people. It is common to see *pukhuris* (ponds) of various sizes all over the Assam valley. Sivasagar, in fact, gets its name from the huge tank built in the name of King Siva Singha. Situated in the heart of the town and spread over 129 acres, the 300-year-old tank was rightly compared to a *sagar* (sea), hence the name of the town—Siva-Sagar. On its bank are three temples (*dols*): Sivadol, Vishnudol and Devidol. The Siva temple is the tallest Siva temple in Assam. All these temples were built by Queen Ambika. In fact, during her time a manual about taking care of elephants, *Hastividyanarva*, was written by Sukumar Barkath in

Situated in the heart of the town and spread over 129 acres, the 300-year-old tank was rightly compared to a sagar (sea) ...

1734; she brought two Muslim illustrators, Dilwar and Dusai, to embellish the book which combines the Mughal-Rajput school with the Assamese Vaishnavite tradition.

Hastividyanarva is a valuable addition to the pantheon of books in India on domestic animals. The restoration and publication of this manual in modern times shows the highly developed art of painting in Ahom times with ample local elements. There was another book like this, though not as famous, on the healthcare of horses.

Incidentally, Ahom noblewomen were well-educated, many of them advised on state matters, and even fought alongside men, as did Mula Gabhoru who joined the battlefield to take revenge on the death of her husband at the hands of Muslim invader Turbak (1532). As King Siva Singha was cautioned with a prediction that there would be a break in his rule (*chatra-bhanga jog*), he made his queens sit on the throne and the queen was called the *bor-raja* (the exalted king) which gave opportunities to strong women like Phuleswari Kuwori, Ambika, etc., to rule. Though Phuleswari, a die-hard Sakta, was accused of angering the Vaishnavites with her diktat, she also introduced women's education and other reforms in the land, as did Ambika too. Also Assamese women were not seen with veils. The absence of dowry in Assamese society is significant while compared to most other parts of the country and is regarded as an empowerment tool for women. The sati system too was never prevalent in Assam.

Near Sivasagar are strewn structures built in the heyday of Ahom rule. At a little distance is the seven-storeyed Kareng Ghar—the royal palace began by Rudra Singha but completed later by a successor. The lower three storeys known as Talatal Ghar, the labyrinthine quarter, are underground and inaccessible today. It is believed that it was connected with the Dikhow river by an underground tunnel as a safety measure in case of an emergency.

Rang Ghar, a two-storeyed pavilion, octagonal in shape and with a shell-shaped roof crowned by an upturned pleasure boat with decorative *makaras* (crocodiles) on both ends, was built during the reign of Pramatta Singha, son of Rudra Singha, for kings and nobles to enjoy sports of various kinds, especially during the Rongali Bihu. Buffalo fight, egg fight, hawk fight, etc., were patronised by the king and the nobles and the winners were handsomely rewarded. Common people were allowed to participate in the fairs and sporting events so that they could have fun (*rang*). Today, in front of the complex the road is full of honking cars but once upon a time the king and his

Doog-doogi pendant
Dhol-biri earrings

nobles used to sit on the upper balcony and from there enjoyed the games enacted on the vast field in front of the Rang Ghar. Boat racing on the Brahmaputra and the big tributaries was also a common sport under them.

Another remarkable structure of the Ahoms was the *maidam* or burial monument for departed kings. The mounds contained not only the king's mortal remains but also his favourite objects of daily use, jewellery, even his favourite consorts, friends, maids and servants too, in order to have a comfortable life beyond. The unornamented *maidams* have a clear similarity to the burial practices for noblemen in South East Asia. In South Korea you can see huge *maidam*-like structures. Gadadhar Singha, Rudra Singha's father, had thirty attendants buried with him but Rudra Singha stopped the practice of *maidam* burial and introduced the Hindu custom of cremation.

Hiteswar Borboruah writes that there was a special class of officials called *maidamiya* to keep an eye on the mounds to prevent looting (Borboruah 2008, 369). However, Mir Jumla opened many of these *maidams* according to an account by a Dutch mercenary soldier, Glanius, as he did not suffer from the superstitions of the local people about the *maidams*.

> ... It being the people's custom to enter with their dead, their best apparel, money and the greatest part of their servants whom they bury alive to bear their master's company...our general Mir Jumla caused several of these tombs to be opened, wherein we found vast treasures, which he carried away with him but which he enjoyed but a small time, for he died soon after (Ibid).

Curse of the tomb? Who knows?

The road network the Ahoms built is being admired even today. It was reported in *The Telegraph* (5 December 2002) that at a conference of the Indian Road Congress in Guwahati, engineers elaborated on how modern technology can be coupled with the Ahoms' system of turning embankments into proper roads, suitable for this flood-prone region. According to the same report, Mr Rutherford, a principal assistant of central Assam, had also written in a journal (dated 1835) that, 'No place in India has been provided with such a splendid system of highways, which was carried uninterruptedly throughout the whole country: from Goalpara, on either banks of the river, to Sadiya.'

'No place in India has been provided with such a splendid system of highways ... from Goalpara, on either banks of the river, to Sadiya.'

The economic prosperity and self-sufficiency of the land had a lot to do with the confidence and discipline imbibed by the Ahom rulers through strict standards, though sometimes it could seem too daunting. Under the economic reforms introduced by officer Momai Tamuli Barbarua, under King Pratap Singha (1603-1641), every man and woman had work demarcated for day and night. After working in the field during the day the women had to spin a certain number of *Muga* reels while men had to make baskets of cane or bamboo. There were officers to check on the performance and if anyone tried to bribe them to avoid the chore, both the giver and receiver of the bribe were severely punished. Every household had to dig a nullah around the house and on the banks bamboo had to be planted. An important building material, Assam has more than forty varieties of bamboo. Along with cane it is used to make fishing equipment like *jakoi*, *khaloi*, etc., trays like *chaloni* (sieve), *khorahi* (basket) and the all-important *japi* (sun-hat). Assam's bamboo is regarded as the best in South East Asia and often sourced for making flutes. Reportedly, flutist maestro Hariprasad Chaurasia often uses those from the Barpeta region.

In Ahom days, it was also compulsory to plant betel nut and betel leaf creepers in the kitchen garden and fruit trees like jackfruit, mango, etc. Today when you journey

Decorative carvings at Talatal Ghar

'The kingdom of
Assam is one of
the best countries
in Asia for it
produces all that
is necessary to
the life of man ...'

through the valley of Assam, the houses in the villages will show clusters of bamboo and kitchen gardens, however small, with these trees.

Indeed as the seventeenth-century traveller-writer Jean Baptista Travernier writes in *Travel in India*:

> *The kingdom of Assam is one of the best countries in Asia for it produces all that is necessary to the life of man, without being in need to go to for anything to the neighbouring states. ... The country also produces an abundance of shellac...they use the lac to lacquer cabinets and other objects of that kind and to make Spanish wax. A large quantity of it is exported to China and Japan...it's the best lac in the whole of Asia for these purposes. As for the gold no one is permitted to remove it out of the kingdom. [It is] kept in large and small ingots which the local people make use of in local trade not taking it elsewhere* (Borboruah 2008, 427).

The Assamese under the Ahoms were fiercely independent and excellent fighters, which the Mughal kings learnt at their cost after getting repeatedly defeated. 'Death is preferable to a life of subordination under foreigners, declared the Assamese monarch, Chakradhwaj Singha,' who defied the Mughals after a brief period of subjugation under an earlier king (Bhuyan 1965, 10). In fact, one of the most debilitating battles between the Mughals and Ahoms was fought on the waters of the Brahmaputra at Saraighat (1671) near Guwahati where the river is very narrow. Today the first rail-cum-road bridge over the Brahmaputra in Assam is named Saraighat Bridge. The hero of the battle was General Lachit Barphukan who used all the weapons of warfare—deception, misinformation, frontal attack—to send Ram Singh, sent by Aurengzeb, packing. The Ahoms were the first to introduce gun powder for warfare in the region too.

The legend of Lachit Barphukan is folklore material today—of how he even sacrificed his own uncle in order to fight for the country. As the story goes, to prevent the Mughals from overrunning the land near Saraighat, he had ordered building of an earthen rampart within the night and the person in charge of the job was his maternal uncle. Late in the night when he came to inspect the progress of the work he found the work far from complete and the labourers resting. His uncle told him that they were too tired to go on. Instantly, Lachit brought out his sword and beheaded his uncle and declared: 'My uncle is not greater than my country,' to set an example that when the

Facing page: The Rang Ghar
was for the enjoyment of sports

The cannons roared in the battles Ahoms fought

enemy was at the door, any laggardness could not be tolerated. Rejuvenated by his patriotism, the labourers worked hard to complete the rampart in time.

There is also the story of how Lachit used his acumen and diplomatic skill to send a message about the Ahom king's capability. Ram Singh on arrival first sent a message to him about evacuation of Guwahati accompanied by a bag of poppy seeds to give an idea of the Mughal force at the doorstep.

Lachit replied that as generals of respective armies they could not negotiate, only their monarchs could. But alongside this he also sent a tube of sand to convey that, 'This is the characteristic of our soldiers'—as numerous as the sand on the bank of the Brahmaputra.

Today, 24 November is celebrated as 'Lachit Divas' or Lachit commemorative day in Assam to pay tribute to his bravery and astuteness.

That the mighty Mughals could be defeated in a naval battle, and that too by a race whose roots lay in a hilly terrain, is significant. When the Ahoms landed in the riverine Brahmaputra valley, they were naturally not used to plying boats. In fact, some accounts say that when Sukapha came downstream to establish the capital at Charaideo he used makeshift plantain plant boats—*bhoors*. In the early years of their reign they found it difficult to dominate the tribes who had arrived earlier; even the Koch kings in western Assam gave them a hard time because they were experts at naval battles and the Brahmaputra was their ally. But they soon learnt the craft of boat (*nao*) building and to use the river to their advantage. Not long afterwards, they built a formidable naval force. The chief commander was called *pani phukan*; below him were other officers and *naobaichas* or sailors. Near Jorhat town there is a village called Naobaicha which must have been a centre of sailors. 'One peculiar feature of the Assamese manner of fighting on the Brahmaputra was the construction of "water-stockades" of a type similar to the ones they built on land. This was a skill known to none else in India' (A.K. Dutta 2001, 131).

Under strict discipline and the stress on activities the Ahoms insisted upon, the people were experts in many fields. There was the *Paik* system that made every able-bodied young man available for labour at the king's command—whether for building roads or fighting as a soldier. No wonder that General Ram Singh, wrote with a note of admiration, 'Every Assamese soldier is expert in rowing boats, in shooting arrows, in digging tranches, and in wielding guns and cannons. I have not seen such specimens of versatility in any other part of India' (Bhuyan 1947, 83).

The Ahoms were egalitarian in their outlook too. When they gave important jobs of administration it was not confined to the Ahoms alone or relatives of other officers. That is why one finds even Muslims in Assam carrying surnames like Bora, Saikia, Hazarika, etc., which are basically indicative of the job profile, such as 'Hazarika'—a man with a thousand people (*hazar*) working under him, 'Saikia'—with a hundred people (*sha*) under him, and so on.

Indeed, the Ahoms had so merged with the land of the Brahmaputra that they soon lost the tag of 'invaders'. Instead, their rule enhanced and developed the socio-cultural life of the land in a great way and established its name as a formidable opponent for would-be invaders.

Orunodoi

It is perhaps in the fitness of things that Sivasagar, which saw flourishing of the language and literature under the Ahoms, should also play a role in the revival of Assamese literature and language. But this time with the help of Christian missionaries! On second thoughts why should it be surprising that even Christian

... the Ahoms had so merged with the land of the Brahmaputra that they soon lost the tag of 'invaders'

The missionaries wrote the first grammar in Assamese, compiled a dictionary, and published the first Assamese magazine called Orunodoi (1846)

missionaries from across the seas lived so harmoniously with local people? After all, the Brahmaputra valley has always nurtured a liberal society taking into its fold different streams of people and coalescing them into the ambience of the river and the fertile valley.

In 1836, a few years after the East India Company extended British colonialism to Assam, the Assamese language was substituted by Bengali as the court language and also as the medium of instruction in schools. That same year, two American Baptist missionaries, Nathan Brown and Oliver T. Cutter, sailed up the Brahmaputra with their families in three large country boats to Sadiya. Though the initial idea was to work with the tribes at the foothills of the Himalayas and also find a route to Burma to spread their missionary work, hostile circumstances of various kinds deterred them. By that time, Brown had discovered something new in Sadiya—the 'sweet' Assamese language and had started learning it. He was soon joined by Miles Bronson, a linguist. They settled down in Sivasagar and opened Assamese language schools. Their popularity made them realise that, '… the Government was following a wrong policy in thrusting Bengali upon the Assamese pupils,' writes scholar

The grounds around Rang Ghar celebrated Rangali Bihu.

Maheswar Neog (Neog 1983, 61). Along with a few liberal and educated Assamese intellectuals, like Anandaram Dhekiyal Phukan, they appealed to the power centre in Calcutta to give Assamese language its due place and subsequently the Assamese language got its rightful place in 1873. Maheswar Neog writes that, 'The American Baptists ...had a great role to play in the collective life of the Assamese people' (Ibid, 63), and that besides bringing news from across the world, '... explored past history of Assam in a magnificent way by bringing out the texts of old chronicles in properly edited form' (Ibid, 66).

The missionaries wrote the first grammar in Assamese, compiled a dictionary, and published the first Assamese magazine called *Orunodoi* (1846)—a treasure house of secular, religious and scientific information. The language used was colloquial and functional. For a magazine of that age, *Orunodoi* was remarkably modern in presentation and content proclaiming from the beginning: 'Monthly Paper, devoted to Religion, Science and General Intelligence.' As Neog writes, '... in contact with English speaking people the Assamese developed modern prose style ... this should be considered the greatest contribution of the Baptists to Assamese literature and culture' (Ibid).

Offering *tamul* paan is integral to Assamese social custom

Jorhat

Jorhat, an hour's journey from Sivasagar, is not on the bank of the Brahmaputra but on a tributary, Bhogdoi. It was always a prosperous business centre as indicated by the '*jor*' (pair) '*hat*' (bazaar)—Macharhat and Chowkihat. In 1794 the weakened Ahom royals decided to shift the capital to Jorhat and the town became a more important centre.

Jorhat is ensconced in the tea country too. In 1885, the British built the Jorhat Provincial Railway to the river port of Kokilamukhghat on the Brahmaputra. Tea chests were loaded on ferries from here on the way to Calcutta to be ultimately sent to England.

Near Jorhat is a community of Muslims who have contributed to Assam's cultural landscape with two musical traditions—*Zikir* and *Jari*. People of different communities, belonging to different religions did not find it difficult to live peacefully in Assam. Some sociologists opine that the salubrious climate, the green valley and the influence of the Brahmaputra woven into the lifestyle have contributed to an attitude of 'live and let live'.

It is interesting to observe that in Assam there is a clear distinction between *thalua* or Assamese Muslims and later-day migrants from erstwhile East Bengal/East Pakistan, now Bangladesh, who arrived by the Brahmaputra and started living on the *char* areas. 'Until the late 19ᵗʰ century Muslims in the Brahmaputra Valley mostly dressed, shaved and worshipped like their Hindu neighbours and eschewed beef.... They asserted that they were the descendents of Indo-Persian warrior nobles who served the Ahom kings' (Sharma, Walkowitz and Weinstein 2011, 99). Some of the Muslims were prisoners of war who had accompanied invader Turbak who was defeated by the Ahoms. They gradually assimilated with the local people and other Muslims who were already there. They also spoke the same language—'Asomiya'. Later-day Muslims who came to the fertile valley were called Mymensinghias—from the district of Mymensingh in present-day Bangladesh.

In the seventeenth century, Sufi saint and poet Hazrat Shah Milan, popularly known as Azan Fakir, came to Assam and preached the message of Islam. He built mosques, introduced congregational prayers and, most importantly, adopted Assamese language and culture and preached the gospel in the language of the people. Reportedly, he even married a local girl. Two genres of music that he popularised were *Zikir* and *Jari* which are still going strong for four hundred years.

Zikir is a group of devotional songs imbued with Sufi philosophy. It is sung with rhythmic steps keeping to the beat of clapping of hands. The compositions

A typical 'Assamese style' house with abundance of fruit trees
(Photo courtesy: Ranjita Biswas)

resemble the *bargeets* in the Vaishnavite devotional song tradition of Assam propagated by Saint Sankardeva in the Middle Ages. Scholars point out that Azan Fakir took a pragmatic approach to spread the message of Islam by using the folk culture of Assam. His message was written and sung in Assamese, such as:

Neriba Kalima dhariba Kalima, Kalima namareguri

(Do not leave Kalima, hold on to Kalima, Kalima is the origin of the Name—Kalima are hymns in praise of Allah and the prophet.)

Until the nineteenth century *Zikir* remained in oral form but Western influence on Assamese literature and its romanticism made scholars take an interest in this tradition and in the process discovered its contribution to the rich folk culture of Assam. Bhupen Hazarika has also used *Zikir* rhythm and ambience in some of his popular compositions.

Though the *Jari* is associated with *Zikir*, there are differences between the two. The content in *Jari* songs is more in the Islamic tradition, like stories on the Karbala tragedy. *Zikir* covers other social aspects too and is more attuned to the local tradition.

Jorhat is also the gateway to Majuli, the famous river island and a seat of Vaishnavism. •

MAJULI

Island of Serenity

From Jorhat the ride to Nimatighat, a river port on the Brahmaputra, is rather tortuous with huge craters and uneven surface dotting all the way. But then if you want to go to Majuli island in the midst of the river, the seat of Vaishnavite culture in Assam, you have to make this worthwhile effort. The island lies between Subansiri river on the north bank and the Brahmaputra in the south. Majuli has quite a few ghats and it depends on where you want to go and then board a particular ferry. Kamalabari ghat leads to the hub of Majuli and so is popular with visitors. It takes one and a half hours to reach the island from this ghat.

As it is the time for the famous *Raas* festival which has Krishna, Radha and the *gopis* or cow herding girls dancing under a moonlit sky, the scene at Nimatighat is chaotic, to say the least. Ferries that look like bigger versions of country boats are getting ready to depart—overloaded with passengers, motorbikes, even cars jostling for space. You board the ferry by walking gingerly on the temporary wooden planks and, as per instructions of a 'helper', obediently descend the few steps to take your seat on the rough wooden benches at the womb of the ferry. Packed like sardines with pilgrims from far and wide across the valley, tourists and foreigners looking on bemusedly at the melee, you wait and wait, for the journey to begin. All the while there is this strange sound that seems to hammer on directly above your head. Motorcycles

অাদৰণি
শ্রীশ্রী কৃষ্ণৰ ৰাসলীলা

স্থান ঃ
ৰাজীৰ গান্ধী
ক্ৰীড়া প্ৰকল্প
কমলাবাৰী, মাজুলী

তাৰিখ ঃ
১০,১১ আৰু ১২
নৱেম্বৰ, ২০১১
(শ্ৰীশ্ৰী টি.ভি.এচ
আৰু নিমাতি কমলাবাৰী
জেত্বী সেৱা)

সন্মিলিত
শিল্পী
সমাজ
মাজুলী

Welcome gate at Nimatighat

Pages 68-69: Ready to leave

Page 68: On the way to Majuli

Pages 66-67: The serene
countryside of Majuli sets
the mood

getting loaded, a veteran traveller informs helpfully. Soon food packets of various kinds appear from the carry bags of the passengers. A scrawny young man comes to collect money for the tickets. Obviously the ferries are on contract basis and there are far too many passengers than permitted.

Majuli has long been known as the largest river island in the world though the fact has been challenged in recent times by an island in South America—Ilha de Marajó on the Amazon in Brazil. Never mind, say the believers, who emphasise that Majuli is the largest 'inhabited' river island in the world. Whatever be the debate, it is less important to the fact that the island's place as a unique cultural and socio-religious centre of Assam, as well as of India, does not brook argument.

On arrival at the ghat, vast tracts of sand on the riverbank greet you. It is the month of November and water of the Brahmaputra is much reduced. However, with a rising riverbed, erosion and flooding have been regular features in Majuli for quite some time now.

Geographical evidence shows that the island was a creation of natural forces unleashed by the river Luit and a tributary, Dihing, between the thirteenth and the sixteenth centuries. In 1750, a huge flood made the Luit move southwards and it joined the Dihing river. 'There is some debate on the year of this event but it has remained emblemed in local folk songs:

Luite erile luitor suti
Dihinge erile kul' (Sarma 1993, 19)

(The Luit left the Luit stream
The Dihing left its bank)

Originally the Brahmaputra used to flow to the north of the island. At that time the island was known as '*Majali*' meaning a plain land between two rivers. In fact, historian J.P. Wade in his book, *An Account of Assam*, compiled in 1794-1800, first used the word '*Majuli*' in the eighteenth century. Before it became an island the landmass was a part of the southern bank of the river.

In historical books Majuli was mentioned as Ratanpur or Ratnapur, a place rich in agriculture which also served as a stopover for boats laden with goods sailing upstream and downstream. Those were the days when the river served as the main thoroughfare—both for ferrying goods and travellers.

As is wont in India—to have a legend associated with a place, hill or river is common and so Majuli too has its own legend about its birth. According to folklore, one day long ago King Arimatta of the Jitari dynasty had gone with his father Mayamatta on a hunting trip. Unfortunately, he mistook his father to be a deer and killed him with his bow and arrow. The sin of patricide was so serious and unheard of that there was no *bidhan* (judgement) by the dharma-sastra or religious text regarding how to do penance for his sin. So Arimatta gave up all his wealth to the Brahmaputra as self-punishment. However, the river did not accept this offer and changed its course; the sandy land the river left behind became Majuli.

Arriving at Majuli, you may have this strange feeling of getting caught in a time warp. Today there are cars, motorcycles, et al, on the road, but the lifestyle is centred around the

Arriving at Majuli, you may have this strange feeling of getting caught in a time warp

satras (monasteries) and their way of life in the best of Vaishnavite tradition introduced by Saint Sri Sankardeva (1449–1568) and carried on by his disciples like Madhabdeva, Damodardeva and others. 'The primary functions of the satra are to initiate disciples, to promote ethico-devotional codes and rules of conduct for the neophytes' (Mahanta 2008, 152). Besides, as D. Nath writes in the book, *The Majuli Island*, '... it is almost an island of the traditional Assamese life and culture. The indigenous art and crafts, the music and dance forms, and the food and dress habits of the indigenous Assamese have considerably survived the stresses and strains of time and circumstances in Majuli' (D. Nath 2009).

Entrance to a *satra*: Reflecting traditional Assamese architecture

Facing page: Waiting for the fare at Nimatighat

The *satras* with their age-old wood-painted doors carved by a special class of people known as *khanikars*, the *bhakts* or followers in white clothes, the sound of the cymbals and drums in the distance as a kirtan is underway—all make it seem like a world apart from the hullabaloo of city life. In a region where Sakti cult is strong this is the only place in Assam perhaps where Durga puja, the autumn festival to pray to the goddess, is not held.

Srimanta Sankardeva was a guru, social reformer and creative genius all rolled into one. Legends say that he could swim across the Brahmaputra. He belonged to a prosperous and educated Bhuyan landlord family from Nagaon district. Even during his student days at the *tol* or residential school, he showed unusual intelligence and a questioning mind. Later, unhappy with the excesses of ritualistic puja he set out to travel to pilgrimage centres in other parts of India at the age of thirty-two in search of a solution to his dilemma.

'Tantrik (sic) rituals with many abominable corruptions were (also) practiced in Assam in the centuries before the birth of Sankardeva ... there can be no denying the fact that that it led eventually to moral decadence, social corruption, perversion and blasphemy' (B.K. Barua 1964, 19).

During his travels Sankardeva came in touch with contemporary thinkers who were at the helm of the rising trend of neo-Vaishnavism which influenced his radical thinking. In Puri he stayed for quite a while and it is said he took Lord Jagannath as his spiritual guru. Later he found Sri Chaitanyadeva of Bengal, a great Vaishnavite guru, thinking along the same lines.

On returning from his pilgrimage, Sankardeva established a shrine which later morphed into the *satra* model, to pray and sing in praise of the Lord. He introduced the doctrine of egalitarianism and simple rituals with the message of '*eka deva eka bine nahi kewa*' (one God, one faith, none else than that One). His other noteworthy achievement was to adapt Vaishnavism to the local ethos and his message was in a simple Assamese language so that common people could understand his doctrine. His magnum opus was *Kirtan Ghosa* with couplets of high literary merit in praise of the Lord and which followers still chant today. Soon his band of believers swelled but his popularity proved to be his enemy. He had to leave his original home due to harassment by some of the local populace, mostly Kacharis and Sakta worshippers. Moving up the Brahmaputra, he and his followers arrived at Majuli around 1517.

This is where he also met Madhabdeva, his chief disciple, who was a trader but knowledgeable about religious texts. He was a Sakta worshipper but engaged in a debate with the guru for days before he admitted defeat and accepted this new doctrine. In Vaishnava litany this encounter is called *mani-kanchan sanjog*—a truly golden encounter: They chose their meeting place at Beloguri in west Majuli to establish the first *satra*. Madhabdeva contributed greatly to the spread of Vaishnavism in the Assam valley and composed the other literary component, *Nam Ghosa*. Recently a centre he established in the Jorhat district, Dhekiakhowa Bor Namghar, a renowned pilgrimage centre, has been recognised by the *Asia Book of Records* for its sacred lamp, first lighted in 1528 and which has been continuously burning for the last 484 years. The people living around the *namghar* have seen to it that the lamp has never lacked oil and wicks. Sankardeva rightly chose Madhabdeva to take forward his doctrine commonly known as *Mahapurushiya* dharma in Assam, referring to these *maha-purush*—exalted men.

The introduction of the *namghar*, a village chapel-cum-congregation point, was a stroke of genius. The *namghars* are not confined to the *satras* alone but every village or community, even towns and cities, have them and they serve as community halls as

Sankardeva established a shrine which later morphed into the satra *model, to pray and sing in praise of the Lord*

well. 'The Namghar combined the functions of a village parliament, a village court, a village school and a village church' (Kakati 1948, 86-87).

The socio-cultural life of the Assamese people is, in fact, entwined with the *namghar*. It serves as a village theatre hall; village elders also assemble here to try cases of social delinquency on the part of any villager. Sankardeva wanted a total social change and not just change in religious beliefs and practices.

Nam-kirtan, devotional singing in praise of the Lord, is an integral part of the village *namghar* in Assam even today. Women are not barred from entering the *namghar* either though they often hold 'women-only' *nam-kirtans* particularly in the month of *Bhadra* (mid August to mid September). In any case, religious fanaticism has never been a characteristic of Assamese society, as Praphulladutta Goswami points out (P. Goswami 2008, 63). John M'Cosh, a medical officer with the East India Company writes in his *Topography of Assama* (1837): 'In Assam no one really bothered to keep up upper-caste status, as a result of which there is greater goodwill among the people here than in people of other parts of India' (Saikia 1980, 146).

The great achievement of Sankardeva, besides his creative legacy, was the way he embraced all people—beyond caste and creed. 'Democratisation had been Sankardeva's lasting contribution to the social system and primarily due to his teaching, caste distinctions have never been rigid,' observes scholar Parag Chaliha (Chaliha 2008, 24). Even Muslims were welcome to his fold, because he looked upon people as equal in the eyes of God and believed '*bhakata nahi jatiajati bichara*' (the devotee does not have a caste or creed). One of his most devoted disciples was a Muslim, Chand Khan, mentioned in Vaishnavite literature as Chand Sai. Other well-known disciples were Norottam, a tribal and Jayahari of the Mishing tribe. Of course, these names were adopted after indoctrination into Vaishnavism. Sankardeva's adherence to equality is easily elucidated in the couplet:

Ram buli tara Miri Asoma Kachari
Garo Bhato Javane Hariro nam loi

(Taking the name of Ram saves all—Miri Ahom Kachari Garo Bhutia—all)

B.N. Datta observes that,

The great achievement of Sankardeva ... was the way he embraced all people—beyond caste and creed.

Many families traditionally dedicate a son to the satra *of their allegiance, much like in the Buddhist monastery tradition*

The Assamese society is very much of an open society, the openness being inherent in the very process of its formation: fusion of different indigenous communities, chiefly of the tribal stock, with waves of settlers and invaders from other parts of India- and even outside as in the case of the Ahoms who have given the land and the people their name (Datta 1980, 45).

Today, even after centuries, Sankardeva's teachings and his simple way of worshipping Lord Krishna are meticulously followed in essence and spirit at the *satras* of Majuli. There are around twenty-two *satras* here now though there were many more previously. Among them, Kamalabari, Auniati, Gorumurah, Dakhshinpat and Samaguri *satras* are more famous. There are *satras* in other parts of Assam too and the one in Patbauisi in lower Assam is equally famous.

All decked up for the *Raas Leela* festival

A *satradhikar* or head rules over each *satra*; the disciples live in huts built in neat rows known as *hatis* in the area dedicated to that particular *satra*. It has its own land, many having been donated by generous kings and powerful landlords in the past. Agriculture is the mainstay of the disciples who manage the fields, rear cows and grow vegetables that they need. Some *satras* allow only celibate disciples or *udasheen* while some allow families, also known as *grihasti*. Sankardeva himself was a family man with wife and children. 'What he stressed seems to be the ideal of the virtuous householder not one who bypasses one's normal activities' (P. Goswami 2008, 60).

Many families traditionally dedicate a son to the *satra* of their allegiance, much like in the Buddhist monastery tradition. Sometimes poor parents send their sons to become disciples too. The young inductees go to local schools but also learn singing,

Dakhshinpat *satra* is a
venerated pilgrimage centre

dancing, scriptures, etc., at the *satra* after school. The celibate-style *satras* like Kamalabari do not allow women performers even today and the roles in the plays or group dances requiring women, such as *Krishna Leela*, are performed by young boys dressed in women's attires.

Sankardeva was a great artiste too. To get across his message he ingenuously used the medium of art and culture. This proved very effective as most of the people were illiterate but could easily relate to the performances and the message of devotion to Lord Krishna.

He wrote plays on the life of Krishna to be performed as *bhaonas* (traditional theatres) in villages. The language used was artificial Brajawali. 'In the matter of form and technique, Sankardeva, to some extent, followed the *Natya-sastra* and added to it some elements from local or regional institutions of folk entertainment' (K.D. Goswami 1999).

The need for staging the plays also gave a boost to local textiles and crafts.

For the first ever *bhaona*, *Chihnajatra*, to be staged, Sankardeva himself painted the 'Seven *Baikunthas*' (celestial abodes) for the screen. At the *satras* you shall also come across mural and miniature paintings which depict Mughal–Rajput influence.

Sankardeva set devotional songs called *bargeets* to classical ragas but with local elements, choreographed dances (*satriya* dance), and introduced percussion orchestras to attract the people to his simple doctrine. The big-sized cymbals as found in Bhutan, known as *bhor-taal*, was introduced as an accompaniment.

Satriya dance today is regarded as a part of the Indian classical dance tradition. Majuli is well-known for masks, cane and bamboo articles and the beautiful handwoven clothes, mainly *mekhela-chador*, produced by Mishing women. The Mishings are a plains tribe. In their language the name translates into 'people of the river'. They are the only riverine tribal community in Assam, having migrated from Arunachal Pradesh.

The Mishings have taken on many of the customs and lifestyles of the valley people. The river is their mainstay so they live in harmony with the water. They build houses on stilts known as *chang-ghars* so that the flood waters do not disrupt their living quarters. The women weave beautiful clothes with colour combinations that reflect a sense of harmony with nature.

In olden times elephant tusk artefacts were common and Majuli had its own ivory craft tradition. Some of the samples like ivory combs and miniature boats can be seen at the museum at the Auniati *satra*. Priceless manuscripts written on bark leaf or *sanchi-paat*, instruments

Miniature painting thrived under Vaishnavite influence

Erosion has taken a toll on Majuli for many years now and ... the island might disappear from the face of the earth altogether

The *'khol'* is integral to Vaishnavite music and dance

used during the *bhaona*, indigenous masks, paintings on wood, huge utensils in brass, palanquins are displayed here too.

Khanikars being versatile artistes were equally skilful in painting, architecture, manuscript-making, mask-making and woodcarving and their produce are strewn across the different *satras* reflecting fine Assamese craftsmanship. The intricately sculpted images of Garuda and other celestial characters, various decorated trays and pedestals, known as *thogi*, for keeping the kirtan, the book of hymns in praise of Lord Krishna, bear testimony to the rich tradition of woodcarving in the land. Manuscript-making, both with and without accompanying painted illustrations, on barks of *agar* trees and cotton folios, is another distinctive tradition of graphic art in Assam.

The *bhaonas* needed actors to put on masks to enact the roles—whether as Ravana, as Garuda or as Hanuman, even as the much-maligned Surpanakha, sister of Ravana. Hence mask-making tradition also thrived in olden times using locally available materials like bamboo, cane and a special kind of clay. But today the art has all but disappeared. Only at the Samaguri *satra*, the family of *Satradhikar* Kosho Kanta Dev Goswami, a Lalit Kala Akademi winner, has continued to produce under his tutelage the masks in the age-old style. There is, however, still surviving a mask-making centre near Nazira between Sivasagar and Jorhat.

Sankardeva's creative legacy is woven into the ambience of Majuli perhaps because in essence it is a cocooned world in the heart of the river. The *satras* remain repositories of 'Sankari' art and culture. The huge complex of Srimanta Sankardeva Kalakshetra in Guwahati also showcases the cultural legacy of the Vaishnavite guru as well as serving as a cultural-cum-research centre.

However, there is also apprehension that these *satras* and the unique heritage will cease to exist one day. Erosion has taken a toll on Majuli for many years now and some experts say the island might disappear from the face of the earth altogether. Records show

Mishing *chang-ghars* are functional and artistic

the landmass in 1950 (the year of the great earthquake) was 1,246 sq. km; today it has shrunk to 480 sq. km. Since 1991 about three dozen villages and some *satras* have been washed away, say reports. The devastating flood in the summer of 2012 has almost split Majuli into two and the island may not survive long at this rate of erosion and flooding, some experts darkly predict.

But faith in Lord Krishna, Majuli's holy position and no less in '*mahabahu*' Brahmaputra is firmly ensconced in the minds of the inhabitants. '*Mahabahu*' is an epithet ascribed to the Brahmaputra to denote its strength. The 2001 census puts the population at 1,53,362. People like Karuna Datta, a resident of Majuli, say with infinite faith and confidence: 'Majuli won't die. If one side of the island goes there's another sandbank rising on the other side. Soon there will be plants and trees and people will shift there. The Brahmaputra never lets us down.'

His words ring in your ears as the ferry makes its return journey to Nimatighat. •

KAZIRANGA

Wild and Beautiful

From Jorhat to the famous Kaziranga National Park via the small town of Bokakhat is ninety-six km and takes just about an hour and a half by the National Highway 37. With its green belt of tea plantations dotted with leguminous tall trees to provide shade, the drive down this road is soothing like a cool lime drink on a hot day, especially for the city-bred.

The national park skirts the hilly state of Karbi Anglong. The Karbis are an ethnic tribe who called themselves Mikirs till the mid 1970s. The term Karbi connotes 'brotherhood'. They have their own folklore regarding the name of Kaziranga. Long ago, there was a young couple, Kazi and Rangai, very much in love with each other. Their match was not approved by their community and one day they went into the forest and disappeared forever. Kaziranga remembers them still.

For centuries now, the name of Kaziranga and the famed one-horned rhino have been joined together by an umbilical cord. Justifiably so as the forest reserve has the highest concentration of the species in the world with three quarters of the entire population on earth thriving here. The unique animal in the ecosystem is protected under CITES (Convention for International Trade in Endangered Species for Flora and Fauna). The word 'rhino' (*Rhinoceros unicornis*) is derived from the eponymous Greek word meaning 'horn-nosed'.

As dawn breaks, the forest department's elephants and mahouts are ready to take the first lot of tourists to the park's Mihimukh area so that they can watch the rhinos up-close. The elephants amble sure-footedly through the elephant grass, measuring up the places they should not step into and occasionally munching on the grass. Then you suddenly smell water. The Brahmaputra and its companion Dipholu are not far away. Silence is the watchword in the park; any disturbance and the animals scurry to hide. The mahout whispers and points out the animals —pigmy hogs, deer, herds of the Asiatic bison with their huge horns looking on suspiciously from beside a *beel* or water from the Brahmaputra trapped in the landmass. During the monsoon these water bodies merge with the Brahmaputra's rain-fed stream. Now, in the distance sandbars speckle the Brahmaputra because it is winter and hence dry. These are seen more and more frequently nowadays as the siltation in the river has increased in the last few decades. In winter, fresh mustard fields make a yellow carpet and migratory birds fly in to enjoy the sun. Ducks and many water-bound birds love the mustard flowers and fish are aplenty too near Kaziranga. The *chitol* fish is famous here but officially it is banned to catch fish inside the forest area.

Of Kaziranga sang Bhupen Hazarika:

Kaziranga mor seuj sopun
Apun Kohora Bagori

Pages 82-83: The one-horned rhinoceros is Kaziranga's pride(Photo courtesy: Shutterstock/LAND)

Below and facing page: Getting ready to start the morning safari

Shimer Luit aru Dipholu apun
Apun moromi Kuthori
Mor Kaziranga khoni ananya (D.K. Dutta 1981, 387)

(Kaziranga is my green dream
Close to my heart are Kohora and Bagori
The Luit in the distance and the Dipholu—they are my very own
As is my beloved Kuthori
My Kaziranga is a rare one)

Kohora, Bagori, Kuthori are different parts of the reserve forest.

While all this drama of flora and fauna plays on, the main attraction, that is, the rhinos, do not seem to care a hoot for the city dwellers on elephant backs who have come to get a taste of an environ that is fast disappearing with the onslaught of urbanisation everywhere. The huge animal, whose weight can be between 1600 kg to 3,500 kg, goes on munching the grass peacefully. The rhino is a herbivore. It is also quite short-sighted. But despite the huge armoured body, it can run very fast and can even attack if it feels threatened when a baby is around.

But human greed and cunning can floor even this formidable looking animal. Poaching is one of the biggest problems forest authorities have to tackle. The main attraction for the criminals is the horn which is nothing but a compact mass of agglutinated hair. Yet it reaps huge profits in the international market, particularly South East Asia, due to the myth about its aphrodisiac qualities. Even other body parts of the animal are in demand.

Between 1983-1989 the number of rhinos killed by poachers stood at 235. The decades-long insurgency problem in the North East also saw an escalation in rhino hunting, experts point out, with much of the money being used to buy arms and ammunitions. Concerted efforts by various agencies helped reduce the number of deaths due to poaching. In fact, Kaziranga was lauded as having one of the best anti-poaching campaigns in the country. Unfortunately, this optimism got a rude shock in the recent couple of years with 2012 being one of the worst years for the endangered species when in Kaziranga around seventeen rhinos were poached. Its other habitats

Life is not easy for the forest guards

Top right: Herds of wild elephants are common to Kaziranga

Pages 86-87: The rhino is the prime attraction of Kaziranga

in Assam, wildlife parks at Pobitora, Orang and Manas, saw four more rhinos felled in the same year by poachers who have resorted to more devious methods to ensnare the animal. In 2013 the first quarter saw twelve rhinos getting killed in Kaziranga, a nightmarish situation for conservationists and park officials. A sudden rise of price in the international market of South East Asia led to rampant poaching, forest officials say. However, new measures to protect the animal have also been taken up.

The horn's demand is sustained by its use in Traditional Chinese Medicine. Chinese emperors with their harems of concubines reportedly patronised the medicine. Yet, researchers reveal that this traditional style of medication prescribed it only for life-threatening fevers and convulsions. Nonetheless, the horn's reputation as an energiser has survived centuries of myth-building and has percolated even into modern times despite international campaigns to demystify these ideas to make the rhino survive in the ever-threatened ecosystem. Continued campaigns by wildlife conservation bodies and cooperation between countries where demand is high and the source country is reportedly having an effect. Yet, the recent instances of poaching seem to vindicate that vigilance is a constant need.

Interestingly, even in the Brahmaputra valley in the olden days the armour-plated *gorh*, local name for the rhino, was a fabled animal for various reasons. In Indian mythology, it is projected as a powerful animal fit to carry the supreme god, Vishnu, on its back.

Perhaps because the unusual projection of the horn resembled the *linga* or phallus, common beliefs centred around its prowess as an ancient sex booster. Moreover, people noticed that the copulation period of the rhino is much longer compared to most other animals. In medieval royal families of Assam and other neighbouring countries, cups made of rhino horn were in great demand as they were attributed with venom-absorbing qualities. Rhino horn rings were also worn by childless couples (perhaps to enhance fertility). In Assamese villages water drunk from a horn was thought to be the 'elixir of life' and especially beneficial to pregnant women. It was also prescribed for, surprisingly, lunatics.

In Nepal, consuming the rhino's urine is supposed to cure diseases like asthma. In Yemen and Oman the horn is carved with intricate designs for dagger handles to lend power and strength to the owner. Taiwan and Vietnam of late also are great consumers of the horn powder, experts say. The Indian rhino's horn is more in demand than that of the African two-horned black rhino, according to K.K. Baruah, former principal forest conservator, Assam. However, it is not only in Asia that the rhinoceros has acquired a reputation for virility. It is often associated with the mythical unicorn, an animal with a horn, that cropped up in many references in ancient Europe and the Middle East. The earliest reference is found in the pictorial art of Mesopotamia.

At one time the Indo-Gangetic plains hosted thousands of rhinos. A seal dating back to 3000 BC, belonging to the pre-Aryan Mohenjodaro civilisation, shows a rhino

Kaziranga is home to a large number of bird species

Top left: The poisonous cobra is just one of the many snake species

inscribed on it. From about 1600 and in the next three centuries it disappeared from the Gangetic plains. The main reason was the loss of plain grasslands to agricultural development, which destroyed the rhino's prime habitat; there were also conflicts with human interests. Sport hunting by both Europeans and local nobles in the late nineteenth and early twentieth centuries added to the depletion.

Looking back at Kaziranga's history, there were hardly twenty rhinos left when the British declared it a game sanctuary in 1916. The credit for its declaration as a protected area goes to Lady Curzon, wife of the then viceroy of India. She had heard from the British tea planters about the fabulous animal and had arrived in Assam (between 1904–1905) to witness for herself this legendary animal. But she was disappointed to find not a single rhino; she only saw hoof prints with three toes, enough to be convinced of the existence of the elusive animal. She urged her husband to look into the matter and find a way to save the animal from becoming extinct. Subsequently, the Kaziranga Proposed Reserve Forest was launched over an area of ninety sq. km in 1905. It was declared as a reserved forest in 1908. More areas were added to the reserved area and in 1916 it was declared a 'Game Sanctuary'. In 1938, the then conservator of forest, A.J.W. Milroy, stopped all poaching incidents and the sanctuary was opened to the visitors. However, the word 'game' seemed to connote 'game' for hunting and to erase that impression, in 1950 senior conservator of forest, P.D. Stracey, changed it to 'wildlife sanctuary'. By 1966, the number of rhinos at Kaziranga had gone up to 366. In 1974, the Indian government declared Kaziranga a national park and offered more resources for conservation of the rhinos. In 1985 it was recognised by UNESCO as a World Heritage Site.

The year 2005 celebrated the centenary year of the Kaziranga National Park.

With the additional area merged mainly from the northern bank of the Brahmaputra, the area of the park has increased from 450 sq. km to 860 sq. km now. The number of rhinos has also increased from 2048 (census 2009) to 2329 (census 2013). In fact, this increase has potential of overcrowding and so relocation plans are on. According to forest department sources, the eight rhinos relocated at the Manas, another World Heritage Site, at the foothills of Bhutan near Barpeta, are doing pretty well. This beautiful park, which is also a Tiger Project area, was denuded of the rhino population as also of other fauna during a prolonged insurgency movement but now it is picking

The year 2005 celebrated the centenary year of the Kaziranga National Park

up with local people cooperating in the effort of resurgence of conservation. Sadly, even though two relocated rhinos gave birth recently, much to the joy of conservationists, three translocated rhinos, from Pobitora, were poached here too.

Though Kaziranga takes pride of place in conservation of the animal, the number of forest guards, dedicated though they are, are woefully few to effectively keep vigil on its five zones—Bagori, Kohora, Agoratoli, Burha Pahar and Northern Range which was created after the addition of the new areas on the north bank near Biswanath. The addition became necessary as it was found that poachers could easily approach through the sandbanks or the north bank in the lean season. The criminals even use electric wires connected to high-tension cables to immobilise the animal. Guns with silencers and even the latest AK-47s are used. Sometimes they cut off the horn even before the rhino is dead. The terrain, not very far from the foothills of the Himalayas, with deep jungles and international borders like Nepal, Myanmar, etc., makes for an easy getaway for the criminals. Media reporters have traced how local criminals cooperate with the mafia of animal smugglers and places like Siliguri in north Bengal are a hub for these activities. Presently, the transit route via Moreh in Manipur is a favourite one, experts say.

Herds of deer are a delight for the eyes in the park

'Who are you?' Kaziranga has one of the largest concentrations of the Asian buffalo

In the afternoon, a jeep safari offers you a better encounter with animals than in the morning as the jeep moves deeper into the jungle, albeit not in the core area. Each vehicle is accompanied by a forest guard. There, a brightly hued red jungle fowl, an ancestor of the domestic rooster, frenetically digs the soil to find worms; it's even time and rose-tinted parakeets create a hullaballoo; on a tree trunk an immobile chameleon looks like a part of the tree's bark but the experienced eye of forest guard Kanak Chandra Nath can make out the difference; after all he has spent more than twenty-five years in this jungle and knows each tree, each brook and cranny in this tropical haven. On the other side of the dirt track you look awestruck at a herd of wild elephants. 'They are getting ready to raid the ripe paddy fields around the villages in the periphery of the park,' Nath whispers. He points out a huge heap of rhino dung. 'They are clean animals; they don't pass excreta randomly but come to a particular spot,' he informs. But that is also a giveaway because the poachers know a rhino is around when they see a dung-heap.

A little deeper into the jungle and suddenly a group of forest guards appear with rifles on their shoulders. Kaziranga is the only reserve forest in the country where guards are allowed to shoot at sight if they encounter poachers. Theirs' is a tough life but they seem happy enough to exchange niceties with visitors. They go into areas visitors are not allowed in and spend days in lonely camps. In the rainy season they are often marooned and so move away in time to safer areas. 'You wouldn't believe, I have seen tiger and deer on the high embankment built for them to escape the flood and not attacking each other. Talk about coexistence!' confides another forest guard. But during the floods younger rhinos, deer, etc., often get swept away and it is not uncommon to hear villagers killing rhinos or feasting on deer meat. During the huge flood of 2012 Kaziranga lost 560 animals including fourteen rhinos. One rhino was poached in the adjacent Karbi Anglong area.

CENSUS REPORT OF KNP

SPECIES	YEAR								
	1991	1993	1997	1999	2000	2006	2007	2008	2009
RHINO	1129	1164	-	1552	-	1855	-	-	2048
TIGER	-	72	80	-	86	-	-	-	-
SWAMP DEER	-	-	-	398	468	-	681	-	-
ELEPHANT	-	-	-	-	-	-	-	1293	-
WILD BUFFALO	-	-	-	1192	-	-	-	1937	-

The forest department keeps tab through census

As the rhino holds centre stage, many do not know that Kaziranga also has the highest concentration of the Royal Bengal tiger—32 per 100 sq. km—compared to any other reserve forest in the country, even taking into account the Tiger Project areas. According to a survey by Aranyak, a local NGO, the figure arrived at (2011) is 106 tigers. The forest department also undertakes its own survey though Aranyak's figure has been more or less accepted. There are also more than 500 species of birds that belong to two endemic bird areas, viz., Eastern Himalayas and Assam plains in the North East. Some 280 species of migratory birds visit the state during the winter.

Other fauna include thirty-four kinds of mammals and forty-two varieties of fish, snakes including the venomous cobra, and many rare, endangered or near extinct species, that inhabit this pristine jungle.

Assam is a part of the Indo-Malayan biodiversity hotspot zone and diversity in flora and fauna is no less reflected in Kaziranga which has around thirty-nine species of animals. The Pygmy Hog, for example, is one of the world's rarest indicator species and Kaziranga has an abundance of it. Assam also has fifty per cent of the country's butterflies. There are five national parks and twenty wildlife sanctuaries within this

Kaziranga is the only reserve forest in the country where guards are allowed to shoot at sight if they encounter poachers

narrow valley. The abundance of flora need not be elaborated. It also includes various orchids like foxtail or *kopou* as called locally and which adorns the Bihu dancer's hair, *bhatou*, a kind of flower balsam yellow in colour, etc.

Travelling towards Guwahati, the capital, by the national highway, you can feel the presence of the Brahmaputra even if it is sometimes at a distance. On the way is Silghat—a river port as the name with *'ghat'* indicates. It was the gateway to the historic Tezpur town on the north bank of the river.

If you continue on the highway without taking the detour to Tezpur, to the right comes into view the lush countryside near Kolong Suti and its tributary, Kopili, in the Nagaon district. This region has nurtured many poets and litterateurs. Poets like Dev Kanta Barua, Sahitya Akademi awardee Naba Kanta Barua, short story writers

... you can feel the presence of the Brahmaputra even if it is sometimes at a distance

like Mahim Bora, have been inspired by this fertile land. Near Nagaon town is also Bordowa, the birthplace of Sri Sankardeva.

Quite surprisingly the area also has a conclave of Sikh community who have all but blended with the Assamese people and culture but retain their religious diktats like donning the turban, wearing the kara and carrying the kirpan. Their forefathers had come to Assam when the third wave of invasion by the Burmese was underway. Ahom king Viswanarayan Singh sought Maharaja Ranjit Singh's help to defeat the Burmese army. Under the leadership of one Chetan Singh, a platoon of 500 soldiers arrived via the Brahmaputra and Kolong river and reached Chaparmukh. After defeating the Burmese, most of the soldiers settled down in the land. Though Singh died, his widow known as 'Mataji' stayed on. Mataji Gurdwara in Borkola village is a popular Sikh shrine in this region. ●

Fishing is a major occupation in the rivers around

TEZPUR

Land of Usha

To reach Tezpur today is easy via the Kalia Bhomora Setu (bridge). But for centuries boats and ferries transported people and goods between the south and north banks of the Brahmaputra from the river port of Silghat.

The Kalia Bhomora Setu, one of the longest river bridges in India at 3.05 km, was opened to traffic in 1987. The name commemorates the wish of Kalia Bhomora Borphukan, an Ahom general, who visualised such a bridge way back in the seventeenth century. As local stories go, the general was very dark, like a black bumble bee (*kalia bhomora*), hence this sobriquet. He had even piled two stone pillars to begin the work on the bridge. A mammoth stone inscription by him at this place bears testimony to this fact. Hence lyricist-singer Rudra Barua sang:

Tahani kalote Kalia Bhomorai luitot putisil khuti
Enete morone phukanok nilehi
Asha gol luiot uti

(Long ago Kalia Bhomora burrowed pillars on the Luit
Then death took Phukan away
And hopes floated down the water of Luit.)

People of the older generation talk about how there were fixed timings for the ferry which plied between the banks; missing it meant getting stranded for the night.

The Kalia Bhomora Setu is one of the longest river bridges in India

Pages 96-97: The Brahmaputra makes the surrounding valley green

'There were plenty of river dolphins in the Brahmaputra those days and they often accompanied us in the ferry,' they reminisce. The number of dolphins, locals call them *shihu*, has gone down drastically for reasons both environmental and manmade as they are hunted for their oil which is supposed to have medicinal properties.

Writer Mahim Bora's landmark short story, *Kathanibari Ghat*, written in 1955, is set on such a crossing by a ferry built upon a chance encounter between a passenger and a family of a woman and her brother. In Bora's pen the beauty of the river, the atmosphere around it and the journey itself coalesce exquisitely and it seems as if the Brahmaputra itself is a character in the story.

On the other bank, a tiger must have been waiting for the hunt in the Kaziranga forest. In the distance, in the sand bars, amidst the kahua and jhow in the dark water of the Brahmaputra, unknown mysteries were winking invitingly. The stars above tried to make out the mysterious presence (Biswas 2012, 11).

The sunset on the river moves him to write, '… the little waves painted themselves with the vermillion of the setting sun and disappeared to some point of rendezvous' (Ibid, 2).

At Tezpur, the river is narrower and the bank is on granite outcrops so erosion as experienced in upper Assam is not such a threat. Tezpur is where another famous river, Kameng, in Arunachal Pradesh, later Jia Bharali in Assam, meets the Brahmaputra.

The town, often referred to as the cultural capital of Assam, is steeped in history. Its reputation goes back to mythical times. This is where powerful King Banasura or Bana ruled. His name crops up frequently in the folklores and oral history of Assam. He is said to have been a great friend of the powerful king Naraka of Kamarupa. Legends say that his daughter Usha was so beautiful that she attracted suitors from far and wide. To protect her from unwanted attention, Bana built a fort surrounded by fire called Agnigarh (fort of fire). Nonetheless, Usha fell in love with a handsome prince but only in her dream. However, she did not know who he was. Her best friend Chitralekha drew the picture of the prince from the description she had narrated and it turned out to be Aniruddha, Lord Krishna's grandson. Scholar A.P. Coomaraswamy calls Chitralekha the world's pioneer artist. Chitralekha through her 'magic' power reached Aniruddha with the message from the princess and, with her *haran-luki* mantra, of abduction and hiding, taught by Narada, smuggled him in; Aniruddha and Usha were married secretly in the *gandharva* tradition, as found in Vedic literature.

When King Bana came to know about it, he was livid. He was a staunch worshipper of Lord Siva and would not allow his daughter to marry a Vaishnavite prince. He imprisoned Aniruddha. When Lord Krishna learned about it, he intervened and there was a great battle between him and Bana. Blood ran in rivulets giving the place the name of Sonitpur; the old name of Tezpur—*sonit* meaning blood. However, in Assamese language *tez* also stands for blood, thus Tezpur connotes the same. Lord Krishna defeated Bana and rescued Usha and Aniruddha.

Some pundits draw attention to the 'Hari-Hara' battle between Krishna and Bana, as is often mentioned in local parlance, to symbolise the conflict between two strains of Hinduism—Vaishnavism (of Hari or Krishna) and Saivism (of Hara or Siva)—each vying for dominance in the valley. In the heart of the town is the Mahabhairab temple where King Bana is said to have worshipped Lord Siva. It is a revered pilgrimage centre as is the Mahabhairabi temple atop a hill dedicated to Goddess Durga.

Whatever be the authenticity of the legend, Agnigarh hillock does exist in the heart of Tezpur town. Today it has been developed into a park called Usha-Aniruddha Udyan. From here the beauty of the Brahmaputra is something worth savouring. However, the sand bars or *chars* you see from the top of the hill even during the monsoon are quite a change from old times; some even have become permanent residences of people. An old man sitting on the bank of the river where the well-known Ganesha temple is located, said philosophically, 'Who knows what *mahabahu* Brahmaputra has in mind? Is he going to leave us and flow more to the south ultimately, as they say in the sastras?' Yes, who knows!

Pages 100-101: Agnigarh muses: 'It's a magnificent river'

Facing page: Figurines on the door jamb: Dah Parbatiya

The doorframe at Dah Parbatiya's ruined temple

That Tezpur had been a seat of cultural exchange with the Gangetic valley from ancient times has been established from evidences of the ruins strewn around the town—artefacts in the beautiful Cole Park, for instance, and near about. Perhaps the best example of it is the door frame of a ruined temple at village Dah Parbatiya close to Tezpur town. Archaeologists establish it as belonging to the Pataliputra School of Art in later Gupta period around the sixth century, and 'in all probability, belong to the period of the Varmana dynasty in Assam' (Ahmed 1994, 155).

It is the oldest sample of temple art in Assam. Two beautiful figures in the doorjamb are identified as Ganga and Yamuna. The ruins also consist of the remains of a brick temple of Siva of the Ahom period, erected upon these ruins. When an earthquake in 1897 ruined the brick temple the older temple came into view.

Excavations at the Bamunipahar hills, sometimes called Ushapahar, in Tezpur, have brought out richly embellished sculptures belonging to the eleventh-twelfth century when the Salashambha dynasty ruled the land. Their capital was Harupesvar, which historians locate at Tezpur. It was the largest temple complex in Assam. The hillock was cut into three terraces horizontally and the entire hillock looked like a temple with a natural rock in the middle, surmise archaeologists.

Today the ruins of the complex talk about a glorious period in this ancient capital. Frequent earthquakes could have brought down the edifice but the door jambs, pillars with beautifully carved figures and *magars* (crocodiles), cry out for attention. As you sit on one of the stone 'seats' to look around amidst the ruins, there is an eerie feeling that they silently prod you, asking, 'Why are we lying here on the floor like this? Take care of us, we beg you!'

Coming to modern times, Tezpur earned the title of Assam's cultural capital due to the presence of some of Assam's most well-known cultural icons here, like the first filmmaker in Assam—Jyoti Prasad Agarwala,

Call for an equal society was Bishnu Prasad Rabha's mantra

Previous page
Top: Bamunipahar: *magar* (crocodile) was a common motif in many structures

Centre: Beautifully carved figures cry out for attention

Bottom: The ruins at Bamunipahar hill talk of a glorious past

Page 104: Richly embellished sculpture at Bamunipahar hill

artiste Bishnu Rabha, theatre personality Phani Sarma, to name a few. This is also where Bhupen Hazarika's musical potential found a fertile ground to bloom under the tutelage of these stalwarts.

Jyoti Prasad Agarwala's ancestors had come from Rajasthan. Charmed by the land they settled down in Tezpur, invested in business ventures and became very prosperous. Marrying into Assamese families the Agarwalas became domiciled in the land. By the third generation the family spawned a great many litterateurs and creative talents.

Jyoti Prasad Agarwala (1903–1950) had gone to London for higher studies but left midway to go to Germany to learn filmmaking. On returning home, he made the first Assamese film, *Joymoti* (1935), based on the play with the same name written by pioneer litterateur Lakshminath Bezbarua. As the story unfolds, Joymoti, wife of Gadapani, was tortured to death by rivals of her husband in the Ahom royal court in the seventeenth century. Getting wind of the conspiracy, Gadapani had escaped and took shelter in the Naga hills. The Ahom court was in shambles at that time and Gadapani was seen as a competitor by the weak king and his cronies. Joymoti's loyalty lay both with her husband and the land. She knew that only a strong person like her husband could put the country back on the right track. On hearing about the inhuman treatment of his wife in an open field, Gadapani came in disguise to request her to reveal her husband's whereabouts. Though she recognised him, Joymoti did not weaken her resolution and ultimately died due to physical torture. Later Gadapani became the powerful king Gadadhar Singha (father of Rudra Singha) and launched the Tungkhungiya dynasty which made great contributions to Assam's socio-cultural life.

Joymoti was, in fact, the third Indian talkie to be made. Making the film was no easy matter. Agarwala had to borrow heavily to finance his film. Also no woman from a 'respectable' family would act in the title role. Ultimately he found a woman ready enough to act—Aideu Handique—but the villagers excommunicated her and her family for the aberration. The film was released but to his great disappointment, the audience's response was lukewarm. Critics say that with exposure to Western culture, Agarwala tried to introduce a more natural style of acting and presentation in the film, but the people, used to theatrical and over-the-top dialogue delivery of that age, could not relate to this modern media.

Yet, Agarwala slogged on and to produce his next film, *Indramalati*, he moved from the town to the family's Bholaguri tea estate and built a makeshift studio 'Chitraban' with locally available materials like bamboo, wood, etc. Today, the only film studio in the North East, Jyoti Chitraban Film and Television Institute established by the state government in Guwahati's Kahilipara area is a tribute to this pioneer.

Agarwala scripted plays, wrote poems, many of which were set to music—a genre known as *Jyoti-Sangeet*. He pioneered using Western orchestra in essentially Assamese musical tradition. His songs often rang with the aspiration for independence under colonial rule, the indomitable spirit of the land and its beauty. The Brahmaputra figured in his lyrics quite frequently as a powerful symbol:

Luitor parare ami deka lora
Moriboloi bhoi nai (Agarwala 2004)

(We are the young men from the bank of the Luit
We are not afraid to die.)

Agarwala scripted plays, wrote poems, many of which were set to music—a genre known as Jyoti-Sangeet

Jyoti Prasad Agarwala was a multifaceted cultural guru

In the heart of Tezpur town the white statue of Agarwala, the Rupkonwar, in front of his ancestral house 'Poki' (at that time it was the only cemented or *poki* house in the town, hence the name stuck), reminds us of his stature as a cultural icon. His death anniversary, 17 January, is celebrated as *Silpi Divas* or Artists' Day in Assam.

Defying death as Agarwala's song reflects, were many freedom fighters in the land. Not far from Tezpur the small town of Gohpur saw the martyrdom of Kanak Lata Barua who at the tender age of eighteen died due to police firing while trying to unfurl the tricolour at the police station at the call of the Quit India Movement in 1942. She wanted to join the Azad Hind Fauz of Netaji Subhas Chandra Bose but was not accepted due to being underage, so she joined the 'Mrityu Bahini' of freedom fighters. Her compatriot Mukunda Kakoty also died during police firing. They were inspired by the sacrifice of Kushal Konwar of Sarupathar near Jorhat who was hanged for trying to derail a train, a charge which he had staunchly denied till the end.

Another great poet-lyricist from Tezpur was Agarwala's contemporary, Bishnu Prasad Rabha (1909–1969), under whose tutelage Bhupen Hazarika took his first steps towards the world of music. Rabha injected new life into Assamese songs and collaborated with Agarwala in his films. Dancer, singer, actor, sportsman and a political activist fighting for the rights of the common man, Rabha was a multitalented personality.

During his student years in Calcutta he was a regular visitor at Tagore's family house. As a member of the college team he took part in an all-India festival for the youth in Banaras. He enjoyed scores of traditional dances of the country at the meet and combined them into a seamless performance. Sarvapalli Radhakrishnan, later to become president of India, was at that time vice chancellor of the Banaras Hindu University. He was so impressed by the virtuosic Rabha that he bestowed upon him the title of 'Kala Guru' or grand master of art, a prefix by which people of Assam refer to him today. The Bishnu Rabha Smriti Udyan, in Tezpur commemorates his contribution to Assamese socio-cultural life.

Another contemporary, Phani Sarma (1909–1978), was known as 'Natasurya' (the sun among the thespians). He acted in *Joymoti* too and later in *Piyoli Phukan* in the title role. Phukan was hanged by the British for allegedly trying to dislodge the colonial power. Sarma was also an acclaimed playwright and director and many of his social dramas spoke of the ills of society and of oppression.

Sarma introduced female actresses for the first time in Assamese theatre at a time when male actors dominated the scene, thus revolutionising the nature of Assamese theatre.

In 1930, Sarma joined the Kohinoor Opera, the first mobile theatre group of Assam. The theatre group travelled all over and, from Dhubri to Sadiya, from the north bank to the south bank of the Brahmaputra, people enjoyed Sarma's performance and his legend grew. The mobile theatre, in fact, is very much alive and popular in Assam even today and much ahead of winter, the production companies are booked solid for the season. They take on more contemporary themes too for the script—from the *Titanic* to Hitler.

Even as early as in 1948, when the euphoria over newly gained Independence was still palpable, Bishnu Prasad Rabha and Phani Sarma produced *Siraj*, one of the iconic Assamese plays, to showcase social reality and the divide between the rich and the poor.

The 'Ban Theatre' of Tezpur was the first modern Assamese theatre hall, established in 1906. Many of the modern Assamese dramas by the triumvirate of Agarwala–Rabha–Sarma were first staged here and that set the tone of the cultural standard for the next generation of Assam.

From King Bana's mythical age to modern times, Tezpur fortunately has managed to hold on to its reputation of natural beauty and serenity heightened by artistic ingenuity. •

The commemorative pillar at the Smriti Udyan calls Rabha a 'master of many harmonies'

Facing page: Rabha was a pioneering dancer

GUWAHATI

From Ancient to Modern

Guwahati is new, Guwahati is old. Pragjyotishpur, Kamarupa—known differently at different times in the past, the capital of Assam looks like a bustling young city where teeming millions, modern houses, shopping malls and eating houses jostle for space. But go back in time a bit and you find that the city is old—*burha*, sitting and contemplating on the bank of Burha Luit about centuries gone by—of kingdoms coming and going, and various races traversing on its ground. It is known as an ancient seat of astrology where pundits at the Navagraha temple at the Chitrachal hill studied the vagaries of the nine planets. Commerce flowed by the river-way of the Brahmaputra, through which also came invaders and fortune hunters in search of the fabulous land.

It is said that the name 'Guwahati' has been derived from two Assamese words—*guwa* or betel nut and *hati* or market. In olden times, they say, there was a huge market near Guwahati selling and buying *guwa* and the name stuck as Guwahati.

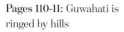

Pages 110-11: Guwahati is ringed by hills

Offering *tamul* paan is integral to Assamese social custom and religious functions

In the Assamese custom, perhaps brought in by Mongoloid migrants, chewing betel nut or areca nut, raw or fermented, by burying in pots under the earth, accompanied by paan, is common both among the rich and the poor. Ahom monarchs employed servants just to prepare the 'chews' for the royal family and this job was given only to trusted people. In fact, the custom has been elevated to such a level that a visitor to an Assamese home is first offered *tamul* paan (*tamul* is another name for betel nut) on a *bota* (bell metal plate on a stand) as a show of respect and hospitality. Even while performing puja and other rituals, offering *tamul* paan on a *sarai* (bigger version of *bota*) is customary.

Echoing the custom, a Bihu song runs thus:

Brahamputrar parare barhamthuri ejupi
Aminu khori lua thai
Brahmaputra devata utuwai ninibo
tamul di matuta nai.

(The holy cotton tree beside the Brahmaputra
The place for us to collect firewood:
O God Brahmaputra, do not flow away.
There's nobody to call you back with betel nut.)

Another version of the *sarai*
(Photo courtesy: Ranjita Biswas)

The Brahmaputra is narrow here, perhaps this is one of its narrowest patches, and as the banks have rocky formation, erosion is prevented. Probably this has also contributed to Guwahati being a preferred place for habitation from ancient times.

Beyond the pages of history, one comes across the name of Pragjyotishpur in epics and mythologies: 'the eastern city of astrology' in place of Guwahati. In the *Mahabharata*, it is said that King Bhagadatta of Pragjyotishpur joined the Kurus against the Pandavas in the great battle at Kurukshetra taking along a huge army of elephants and Kirata soldiers. According to *Kalika Purana*, Brahma created Pragjyotishpur as a city equal to the city of Indra, the king of *devtas* or gods.

The earliest kings of this land were referred to as *danavas* or demons and *asuras* or monsters as they came from non-Aryan stock. 'The earliest organized political system of prehistoric Assam (Pragjyotisha) is attributed to the *danavas* of whom Mahiranga

is referred to as the original monarch' (Chaliha 2008, 15). A hill called Mairang near the Beltola area in Guwahati is associated with him. His descendent, Ghatakasura, was overwhelmed by an adventurer, Naraka, probably an Aryan, who arrived from Mithila. Naraka was the father of Bhagadatta from the *Mahabharata*.

Naraka is attributed with great qualities and was the first to 'import' Aryan culture into the land which was often referred to as *mlecha* (non-Aryan) country in a derogatory manner by people of the Gangetic valley. But some other pundits say Naraka was non-Aryan. Indeed, he is often referred to as Narakasura.

However, Pragjyotishpur was not just a place but an expanded area. Different sources '... clearly testify that Prag-jyotisha was a vast kingdom in the eastern region

[that] included the greatest part of modern states covered by the Northeast region together with the Bengal districts of Jalpaiguri and Cooch Behar, Bangladesh districts of Sylhet, Rangpur, Bogra, Mymensingh, Dacca and Tripura and a part of Patna also' (Ahmed 1994, 3).

The name remained so till it took on the name of Kamarupa in the third century as mentioned in *Markandeya Purana*. Presently the district of Kamrup of which Guwahati is the district headquarter still bears that ancient name. As the story goes, Kamadeva, the god of love, was sent by the *devtas* to put an end to Siva's mourning after the death of his wife Sati; he was roaming around the world with her body on his shoulders and was not paying attention to his duty, as one of the triumvirate of Brahma-Vishnu-Maheswar

A monsoon evening over the Guwahati sky

Following pages: The hills are ancient, the city is new

(Siva), of looking after the cycle of creation, preservation and destruction. Kamadeva let loose his arrow of love and passion to disrupt Siva's preoccupation. At this Siva became so angry that his third eye opened and its fire burnt Kamadeva to ashes. But his wife, Rati, pleaded and prayed so fervently for forgiveness that Siva relented. According to mythology, he told her, 'There is only one way. There is a place in the east of India where he can get back his form and beauty.' So, she came here along with the ashes and Kamadeva found his *rupa* (form) again; hence the name 'Kama-rupa'.

Nirmal Prova Bordoloi observes that the name Kamarupa may indicate an association with Tantricism. 'The extremely ascetic way of attaining *moksha* by the Saivaites merging with saktaism seem to be symbolically combined in this tale. *Kama* or sexual desire found *rupa* or embodiment here; hence *kamarupa*. It hints at secret sexual rituals endorsed under Tantricism' (Bordoloi 1986, 375).

However, as is obvious, many of these stories are rooted in myths and interpretations. The historical period of Assam begins in the fourth century, when the name Kamarupa takes over from Pragjyotishpur at the beginning of the Varman dynasty.

The Varman dynasty had thirteen rulers starting with the founder, Pushyavarman, a contemporary of the powerful Gupta dynasty. Among them, Bhaskarvarman (AD 600-650), was the most famous. He was a friend of Emperor Harshavardhana of Kanauj. At the great religious festival 'Bauddha Maha Mela' in Kanauj, Bhaskarvarman was given the highest place of honour among other royal invitees.

A Chinese *paribrajak* or traveller and Buddhist pilgrim, Hieu-en-Tsang, spent a few years at the court of Kanauj and Nalanda University. At Bhaskarvarman's invitation, Hieu-en-Tsang came to Kamarupa. Though the king was Hindu, he was tolerant of other religions. The Chinese pilgrim spent about one month in the royal court. The account of his travel to Kamarupa (*Si-Yu-Ki*) portrays a valuable picture of the land of the Brahmaputra during that period. He said that the capital was five miles in circuit; though trees were abundant people valued and esteemed them. Jackfruit trees and coconut trees were cultivated and much prized. Water from the river and the lakes flowed round the towns. He also observed that they adored the *devas* and had 'no faith in Buddha'; hence from the time of Buddha they had not built a single *sangharama* or Buddhist temple where priests could assemble, though 'it was in Assam that Tantric form of Buddhism originated' (D. Dutta 1989, 18).

Tantricism, in fact, is associated with Pragjyotishpur from ancient times. Edward A. Gait says that it, '... is interesting in connection with the reputation which the country has always held as a land of magic and incantation with the view that it was in Assam that the Tantric form of Hinduism originated' (Gait 1933, 15).

The Kamakhya temple is regarded as the most sacred *pitha* or pilgrimage centre for Tantric worship where 'Sakti' or woman power reigns supreme. As the legend goes, when Siva was traversing the earth with the body of Parvati or Sati, the gods appealed to Vishnu to find a solution. Vishnu sent his *sudarshan chakra* (discus) to cut the body parts of Sati one by one; each place where a body part fell became a pilgrimage centre. In Kamakhya, atop the Nilachal hill, fell the private part—*yoni*—and became a most revered pilgrimage centre of the Sakti cult.

The sacredness associated with Kamakhya and the commanding position over the Brahmaputra, from where it looks like a white *chador* or blanket spread up to the horizon disappearing into the blue hills beyond, made present Guwahati a preferred capital for different dynasties.

King Naraka is credited to have built the first temple of Kamakhya. By that time, according to a *Puranic* story, Naraka had become so powerful and arrogant that he even dared to ask Goddess Kamakhya's hand in marriage. She pretended to accept the offer on condition that he built a temple for her within a night. Naraka had almost completed the task when the terrified goddess took help of another goddess, Bhairabi, to avoid the catastrophe. She took the form of a cock and crowed, heralding the first hour of dawn before the actual time. Obviously, Naraka could not marry Kamakhya.

However, the temple slowly decayed with time and the present one was built by the powerful Koch king, Naranarayan (1540-1586) who ruled over vast tracts in western Assam as well as north Bengal which was also known as Kamata kingdom.

There is another legend relating to Kamakhya and the Koch kings. Apparently there was a rumour that after sundown one should never try to enter the temple or go near about as the devi was supposed to descend and dance by herself. Naranarayan's brother Sukladhvaja or Chilarai as he was known locally (so named because he could swoop down on the enemy like a powerful *chila* or kite), was a powerful general. He was curious to verify this rumour and one day he peeped through a hole and saw the devi dancing inside the temple. The devi found out instantly and cursed the royal family with dire consequences if any of them ever dared to step into the premises of the temple. As a priest of the temple elaborates on various legends around Kamakhya, he tells the story of Chilarai claiming that descendents of the Koch royal family have never visited the temple to this day. There is no way to verify it, so you accept it at face value.

To reach the sanctum sanctorum of the temple you have to climb down a few ancient-looking stone steps. It does not have a deity as such but a *garva* (womb) shaped like a woman's *yoni* where there is a constant flow of water.

This peculiarity has also added to the devi's comparison to a woman and a mother —'ma'. In the month of *Ahar* (mid June to mid July), the temple is shut down for four days for the festival of Ambubachi (*aamati* or *shath* in Assamese language). Writes Sivanath Barman: 'In Sanskrit *ambu* means water and *wasi* means blooming or flowering; the Hindus believe during Ambubachi the mother earth goes through a menstruating period' (Barman 1982, 43). As per custom, Kamakhya becomes untouchable. In many homes of Assam, particularly in the villages, a woman during the menstruation period is not allowed to enter the kitchen and generally keeps herself scarce from daily chores. During

Ambubachi period, agricultural activities like digging, ploughing, sowing or transplanting are prohibited in Assam.

After the period of closure is over, the priests at Kamakhya temple distribute red pieces of cloth symbolising the menstruating period among the devotees. Barman has an explanation for this belief. Due to the incessant rain during this period, the stone at the sanctum sanctorum gets washed off the red vermilion smeared on it and the vermilion flows with the water giving it a red colour. Devotees have interpreted this as otherwise from ancient times.

R.M. Nath also writes: 'The natural spring flowing out of the rocky hill on the bank of the Brahmaputra river oozed out reddish water due probably to the fact that the rock contained red-haemalite. The people living near about this area were known by the general term as Kha-chais' (R.M. Nath 1948, 4). Later the term changed to Khasias, and then Khasis of Meghalaya as we know them today.

Nath also explains the phenomenon of believing in Goddess Kamakhya menstruating thus (Ibid):

Page 118: Waiting to go to Umananda

Pages 118-19: Guwahati's landscape from the Nilachal hill

Pages 120-21: The Kamakhya temple is a venerated *sakti-pith*

Mythological figures greet you at the Kamakhya temple entrance

At the point at which the water oozed out from the rock at its foot there was a natural fissure conical in shape about nine inches in length and 15 inches in width and reddish pink in colour looking very much like the genital organ of a woman. This further strengthened the belief that Mother Earth menstruated through this fissure at the peak time of cultivation ... this place was called Ka-Mei- Kha (mother-water-course). The Hindus named the place Kamakhya and worshipped it as the genital organ of the Supreme Mother (Kha as verb means give birth to).

The symbolism reminds us of R. Briffault's writing: 'The identification of earth with women

pervades the thought of all stages of culture, and pages could be filled with illustrations of the universal equation' (Barman 1982, 47).

It has been a long journey

During Ambubachi, which is regarded as extremely holy by Sakti worshippers, a huge mela gets underway at the temple site. People from all over the country, even from as far as Nepal, come to pay obeisance. The majority of the pilgrims and sadhus, however, come from neighbouring Bengal where Sakti worship is equally prevalent—as Kalighat temple and Durga puja festivals illustrate.

You ask some of them sitting under an overcast sky why they come to the Ambubachi mela. 'We come here every year,' says Sudharani, a sixty-plus woman from Bankura district, West Bengal, adding, 'This is the time to be here, to pray to our Ma Kamakhya.' A group of sadhus in red attires and matted hair wait with infinite patience for the temple's door to open. At the entrance to the gate long queues of people, some with babies in arms, wait too. Faith, you decide, is something very personal. It also

... the Khasis
say Kamakhya
is a Sanskritised
version of
Ka Mei-kha,
signifying the
mother from the
father's side, and
highly respected

keeps people going in daily life with its many problems, a sadhu says. Surprisingly, he was a professor of science in Bengal before he gave it all up and has now made Kamakhya his home.

Kamakhya is an important entity in the Hindu pantheon of goddesses. But the Khasis of the neighbouring Khasi and Jaintia hills, now named Meghalaya, have always claimed that she was their goddess whom the Hindus took into their fold later. The Khasis are of Austric origin and were one of the earliest migrants to the Brahmaputra valley and follow a matrilineal social system. Scholar-linguist Bani Kanta Kakati even found the name Pragjyotishpur to be of Austric origin, contending that it does not have any religious connection but relates to topographical features of the land. He finds resonance of the name in the Austric words '*Pugar-Juh-tic*' meaning a region of extensive high hills which was later Sanskritised into Pragjyotishpur (Kakati 1948, 6).

Likewise, the Khasis say Kamakhya is a Sanskritised version of *Ka Mei-kha*, signifying the mother from the father's side, and highly respected. Another myth says Kamakhya hill is where the Khasis halted during the journey from *Makachiang* (Himalayas) to their present home. The Hindus later built a temple here and adopted earth-mother worship as Sakti worship. The word 'Khasi', by the way, is broken into *kha* or born and *si* or ancient mother (Bareh 1967, 10).

Guwahati or Pragjyotishpur boasts of quite a few pilgrimage centres even in the midst of the Brahmaputra. An ancient temple devoted to Siva is at Umananda or Peacock island as the British called it. Legend has it that it was created when Siva burnt Kamadeva to ashes. Even the hillock on which the temple rests is called Bhasmachala hill (hill of ashes). Pilgrims who come to visit the Kamakhya temple also ritually visit Umananda, signifying the close relationship between Siva and Parvati or Sakti in Hindu mythological beliefs. Ferries go from near Uzanbazar ghat in Guwahati at regular intervals to Umananda. It has one of the earliest brick-built structures built by Gadadhar Singha. The island hosts the rare Golden Langur though they are rather elusive. For a better chance of spotting the primate you have to go to the Manas National Park near the Bhutan border.

At Aswaklanta in north Guwahati, there is a temple constructed by King Siva Singha on the bank of the Brahmaputra. Legend says that Lord Krishna, while on his mission to annihilate Narakasura, stopped here as his horse was tired (*aswa* is horse and *klanta*

Facing page: Ritual at the holy pond before entering the temple

means tired) and that the hoof marks are still there on the stone surface to prove it. Another legend says this was where Krishna rested his horse while taking along Rukmini from Sadiya. There are also some other stories regarding the horse that was attacked near this temple. One such story is that its name should have been 'Aswakranta' (literally, horse attacked) and not 'Aswaklanta'. Earlier there was a *kunda*, a place of sacrifice, near the temple. This has since disappeared, perhaps eroded by the Brahmaputra.

From those uncharted mythical times to modern times is a big jump indeed but Guwahati retains that aura of a vast habitat carrying on through the ages. Sometimes people wonder what is so ancient about the place, except for temples like Kamakhya or Navagraha, because what you see around are constructions mainly erected during the Ahom period. But you have to remember that this region falls under an active seismic zone and has gone through many natural disasters, particularly earthquakes, and whole towns might be lying below the present city. This is no idle speculation as the excavation of the Ambari site proves.

Ambari is in the heart of the city near Dighalipukhuri. While undertaking construction work labourers discovered beautiful statues of gods and goddesses. Further excavations tentatively suggested outlines of an older town buried beneath. Digging up the whole area would be next to impossible for obvious reasons. It would mean destroying an area with some of the most important buildings and housing localities. The statues already found at the Ambari

site are now on display at an annexe of the state museum. According to the Archaeological Survey of Assam, Ambari's township could be more than two thousand years old. Litterateur Birendra Kumar Bhattacharyya writes that a group of Pune archaeologists led by late H.D. Sankalia,'... felt that the Ambari pottery discovered in the lowest layer of the site was different from the wares found in other sites in India and might hold the key to the discovery of a distinct Brahmaputra valley civilization' (Bhattacharyya 1994).

Even Dighalipukhuri as is seen today was a different entity in the past. The pond was originally supposed to have been dug straight out from the Brahmaputra. The pond or *pukhuri* derived its name because of its half-a-mile length (*dighal*). It is one of the most ancient artificial ponds and dates back to several centuries. Historian Rai Bahadur Kanaklal Barua states that, 'Dighalipukhuri is as old as the epic *Mahabharata* itself' (K. Barua 1966, 119). Legend also has it that the pond was actually created by Bhagadatta by digging a canal from the Brahmaputra.

Apart from the plethora of legends and myths surrounding Dighalipukhuri, it was actually during the era of the mighty Ahoms, that the real significance of the pond came to the fore. It has been safely conjectured that Dighalipukhuri was a channel and in all probability was used as an ancient boat yard as well as an inland port for warships. In gradual course of time, the mouth to the Brahmaputra was closed, with Dighalipukhuri itself being insulated from the main river. Ultimately, during the British colonial times, the bulk of the northern end of Dighalipukhuri was filled up on which the present-day Circuit House and the Gauhati High Court were constructed.

As scholars and sociologists have pointed out, Assam was never a land of religious intolerance or caste-related rigidity. If some rigidity developed later, especially among the Brahmins, it was brought about by later migrants. A good example of spiritual coexistence is Hajo (from '*ha gojou*' meaning highland in Bodo language), an hour's drive from Guwahati, which is a place of pilgrimage for Hindus, Muslims and Buddhists

Sadhus congregate for Ambubachi

Facing page: Sculpture on the wall of the Kamakhya temple

Following pages: Umananda island is an ancient pilgrimage centre

alike. Hindus offer prayers at Hayagriba Madhava temple on the Manikuta hill devoted to Lord Krishna; Muslims pray at the Poa Mecca where a *poa* of earth (equivalent to one fourth of a *ser*, the old unit of measurement) was supposed to have been brought in from holy Mecca; Buddhists believe that Lord Buddha attained nirvana here. The Bhutias from nearby Bhutan still come here on pilgrimage in the winter. It is true that the Brahmaputra valley had a strong tradition of Buddhism in the early days which got submerged by the rising power of Hinduism later.

Hajo is also famous for bell-metal work (*kanh*) as is Sarthebari which is not very far from Guwahati. Assamese people swear by this metal and prefer it to brass utensils for everyday use.

Today, the spinning and weaving centre is concentrated at Sualkuchi, thirty-five km north of Guwahati. You will find that most of the weavers, overwhelming numbers being women, are Bodos for whom weaving is an age-old skill. Even as you approach the place the '*khat ... khat ... khat*' sound from the looms called *saal* greets you from afar.

The courtyards of every house in the area depict women busy at work—either reeling threads or preparing the threads to put in the loom. Thousands of workers are concentrated around this cottage industry. The process, handcrafted from stage one to the finished stage, is highly compartmentalised, with each specialising in a particular segment. Women like Arati Boro have come from nearby Goreswar. 'We are taught weaving from a young age. Now Sualkuchi has given us an opportunity to earn a living out of it; our money also helps the family to survive.' Ethnically, Arati is a Bodo. It is believed that the art of silk weaving arrived in the North East along with the migration of the Bodos.

The workers devote a minimum of eight hours a day but the payment is according to how fast they can turn out a piece; payment also depends on the intricacy of the design (*butas*). Usually it takes about a week to turn out a finished piece. Life is not very comfortable though. Even in the hot summer they cannot afford the luxury of a fan since the delicate threads tend to break under the blast of the rotating blades. Fortunately, due to the continued patronage of Assamese people of this homespun product and with new export opportunities opening up in the market, the art of weaving in this region has not died down like many age-old handicraft traditions in India.

As per reports, there are 23.22 lakh people employed in weaving and allied activities at present, making it the biggest cottage industry in the state. Sualkuchi itself has more than 17,000 looms.

After Assam came under the British, the hill station of Shillong (now capital of Meghalaya) was chosen as capital of undivided Assam. But Guwahati saw major developments like establishment of the Cotton College in 1901. Students prior to its launch had to go to Calcutta for higher studies. It was also the railhead for access to the North East. At that time undivided Assam was a huge landmass. People from outside as well as from the north bank travelled by railway upto Amingaon on the north bank and then took a ferry to reach Guwahati. In fact, until the Saraighat rail-cum-road was built in 1962, this is how people commuted between the banks of the Brahmaputra. Even today, the ferry on the Brahmaputra is a popular means of transport between the two banks.

Even today, the ferry on the Brahmaputra is a popular means of transport between the two banks

One of the streams of the Brahmaputra river, now encircled by land, has formed Deepor *beel*, a 4,000 hectare freshwater lake. You can see it in the distance on the way to the city's airport. The lake is listed as a wetland under the Ramsar Convention. Wetlands listed as a Ramsar site are protected and filling of the lake water with earth or any change is prohibited under the international law. In winter, thousands of migratory birds land here. More than a thousand fishermen's families sustain themselves on the banks of the *beel* which is also rich in biodiversity. Assam has around 187 species of freshwater fish and of them at least fifty are available in the Deepor *beel*.

Gauhati, the anglicised version of Guwahati, Pragjyotishpur, Kamarupa—call it by any name, but this ancient city still remains the gateway to the North East, as it was in the past. •

From old to modern, the Luit is witness to all

GOALPARA
Song of the Elephant

Pages 132-33: The fertile land has attracted many migrants

The *Bagurumba* dance has often been compared to a butterfly dance
(Photo courtesy: Pitamber Newar)

Leaving behind Guwahati the Brahmaputra moves towards western Assam and Dhubri from where the river enters Bangladesh. At one time, this area west of Guwahati was the domain of the Koch kings whose capital was in Coochbehar, now in West Bengal.

Monsoon rain was lashing the countryside on the way to Dhubri some 300 km away from the capital. The highway lay like a path to an unknown destination with tall sal trees keeping vigil on both sides. The rain stopped suddenly and the landscape looked like a freshly bathed maiden dressed in green while the Garo hills hidden in the mist and clouds tried to get a glimpse of her.

From time to time you pass Bodo villages where women in their beautifully woven *dakhnas* walk on, ignoring the shower. This is the land of the Bodos. Racially they are Mongoloids (Kiratas). Suniti Kumar Chatterji in his monograph, *Kirata-Janakriti*

(1951), called the Bodos Indo-Mongoloid, thereby defining their origin as well as their Indian connection. The Kiratas are mentioned in many Sanskrit and old Assamese texts as also in the *Ramayana* and the *Mahabharata*.

The Bodos, pronounced 'Boro' locally, is more indicative of a linguistic homogeneity than of a particular tribe. Within its fold are tribes like Kacharis, Garos, Mech, Rabhas, Lalungs, the Tipparas and Hajongs of Tripura, etc. They are found upto Sadiya in eastern Assam as also in Arunachal Pradesh and north Bengal. The Koches were actually of Bodo stock according to Chatterji. They later adopted Hindu religion.

The Bodos were one of the earliest migrants to Assam from the great plains of China. According to R.M. Nath:

The first batch of the Bodos who migrated to Assam came from a place situated at the confluence of two rivers, Dila-ubra (big water) and Changriba (small water) due to that area being disturbed and converted into a desert by an earthquake, This was very likely a part of the present Gobi desert (R.M. Nath 1948, 16).

Hurry up before the rains come

Until the Ahoms came the Bodos were the dominant tribe, especially in upper and middle Assam

Other experts too say that the Bodos migrated from north-west China and Tibet down the course of the Tsangpo and Irrawady, entered Burma and subsequently India's North East. According to B.K. Barua, the Bodos divided into different groups and spread all over the valley. They surged down the great bend of the river at Dhubri and settled down there. Another stream set up home by the Kapili river near Nagaon district; yet another went to the Garo hills. Those entering from the eastern side set up powerful kingdoms like the Kachari kingdom near Dimapur (now in Nagaland) and the Chutia kingdom. Until the Ahoms came the Bodos were the dominant tribe, especially in upper and middle Assam (B.K. Barua 1969, 6).

'... scholars have noticed that the Bodos, generally regarded as belonging to the Tibeto-Burman race and much more numerous and stronger than others [like early migrant tribes] and with much more contributions to the Assamese culture' (Shastri 2002, 9).

In western Assam, the sixteenth and seventeenth centuries were glorious years for the Koches with kings like Naranarayan who contributed greatly to the cultural and social upliftment of the lower Brahmaputra area.

Centuries of living in the land have made the Bodos adopt the Assamese script while writing. Bodo language has been the medium of instruction in the Bodo-dominant areas since 1963.

The Bodo language is rich with a vast range of oral literature comprising folk songs, folk tales, ballads, etc. Reflecting their rural lifestyle, the emphasis is often on the grain storehouse and cows.

Folklore research scholars at Gauhati University reveal that the Bodos have great skill in constructing irrigation canals and earthwork embankments for diverting water from the riverbeds to the rice fields.

Just like the Assamese, Bohag Bihu, which they call Baisagu, and Magh Bihu, known as Damasi or Damahi, are important community festivals for the Bodos. Dance and song are integral to the festivities. The Bodos have their own musical instruments to liven up the performances: *siphung* (flute), *gogona* (mouth organ), *kham* (drum), *serenza* (indigenous violin), to name a few. One of the most graceful dances of the Bodos is the famous *Bagurumba* performed by Bodo maidens. Attired in their colourful

The Naranarayan bridge is named after the great Koch king

According to popular belief, 99,999 Sivalingas were engraved here by sage Vyasa who wanted to make it a second Kashi ...

ethnic dresses, dominated by yellow, the colour of ripe paddy and mustard flowers, they dance as if floating in the air and sometimes look like butterflies with their *arnai* (*chador* for upper body) flapping in the wind.

The most important religious festival for the Bodos is Kherai puja, an annual event for welfare of man and animal, particularly paddy, to ensure a good harvest. A must for the occasion is the *deodhani* (female shamanistic dancer) who is regarded as a conduit through whom their prayers to the gods and goddesses are delivered.

The Bodos on the north bank of the Brahmaputra narrate their origin of creation as a race by worshipping Bathow, the supreme God, who represents the five basic elements of creation. Bathow is also referred to as Sibrai (Siva) and his consort as Siburoi (Parvati) who created the universe. They believe that the Hindus' worshipping of Siva, whose abode is in the Himalayas, originates from their Bathow.

It is interesting to note that courtyards in Bodo households have an altar for *Khamaikha* (Kamakhya, the Mother Goddess) which harks back to the devi's place in the tribal psyche. They also observe Ambubachi and call it '*amthisua*'. The position of women is egalitarian in the Bodo society. They work alongside the men in the fields.

Driving on, the third rail-cum-road bridge over the Brahmaputra at Jogighopa and Pancharatna hill, named Naranarayan Setu in honour of the great Koch king, now comes into view. Before reaching here, you have to take a detour of around fourteen km to reach Goalpara town on the bank of the Brahmaputra. The famous Sri Surya Pahar (hill) is on this path. The hill is representative of three religions—Hinduism, Jainism and Buddhism—which existed here at different periods of time. It is one of the rare places where Surya, the Sun God, was worshipped in ancient Assam. There are numerous *Sivalingas* strewn around too. According to popular belief, 99,999 *Sivalingas* were engraved here by sage Vyasa who wanted to make it a second Kashi (present-day Banaras).

This part of Assam had also gone through Buddhist influences, particularly when it was under the Palas of Bengal. As evidence is a votive stupa, resembling a bell, as also around twenty-five stupas. After the Palas under whom Tantric Buddhism flourished in Bengal, the orthodox Senas came into power in the eleventh century and the persecuted Buddhists often took shelter in the Goalpara district and contributed to the development of Buddhist art in Assam (Ahmed 1994, 74).

Facing page: 'This is my land'

The Mahamaya temple
symbolises Sakti worship cult

This is also the only place in the North East where the remains of Jainism can be found. There is a carving of Adinath, the first Tirthankara of the Jains, as also other Jain carvings, dating back to the ninth century, in the hills.

On the way to Dhubri is the famous Mahamaya *than* (temple) of Bagribari, next in importance to Kamakhya as a Sakti worship centre.

The town of Gauripur is an hour's drive away from Dhubri. The name immediately rings a bell for you: It reminds you of a legendary filmmaker and of elephant songs. The royal family of Gauripur has given Indian cinema the celebrated Pramathesh Chandra Barua, the original Devdas, writer and director; folk singer Pratima Barua Pandey of '*Mahut Bandhu Re ...*' fame, and also Parbati Barua, reputed to be the only woman 'elephant catcher' in India today.

P.C. Barua (1903–1951), as he was known, was a pioneer, actor, writer, director, rolled into one at a time when Indian cinema was evolving. 'He introduced a daringly new style of acting-low-key, restrained, understated- in films that stood the test of time' (Vasudev 2008, vii). He was one of the founding members of India Film Society in London in

1948 and was the first Indian and non-European to become a member of the British Kinematograph Society.

The Barua family has spawned many illustrious sons and daughters though some are less known. For example, P.C. Barua's sister, Nilima Barua, was a collector of artefacts of the Goalpara region. Her textile collection is particularly remarkable. The other sister, Niharbala Barua, wrote a series of articles titled *Prantabashir Jhuli* (Tales from beyond, 1952) in the Bengali literary magazine *Desh* on the region's history and culture.

Pratima Barua's songs with a strong accent on the folk tradition of the land, known as *Goalparia Loka Geet*, came into focus after her talent was recognised by Bhupen Hazarika when he first heard the young girl's voice in 1955 and was given an opportunity to record this genre of music for All India Radio, Guwahati. He also used her as playback singer in his film *Era Bator Sur* (Songs of the Deserted Path, 1956). By the time she brought out the LP disc '*Mahut Bandhu Re*' with five solo songs and one duet with Hazarika, she had not only become famous but more importantly, she had injected new life into a folk tradition which was on the wane. Folk scholars also point out that along with the folk music she helped revive the language of the erstwhile Goalpara region, presently comprising the four districts: Goalpara,

The 'eyes' at Mahamaya *than*

Bongaigaon, Kokrajhar and Dhubri. The language contains nuances of both Assamese and Bengali and is often called *desi bhasha* (native language); at one time it was almost going through an identity crisis, hinged between Assamese and Bengali, at least in the eyes of the people outside the district. But it has always been known as *Goalparia bhasha* locally. Pratima Barua who passed away in 2002 has left behind a legacy which has gone from strength to strength with time.

'*Mahut Bandhu Re*' signifies the close affinity between the elephant and the man. This is a unique form of songs sung by *phandis* (elephant catchers with their *phand* of jute rope). Their profession is to catch wild elephants for domestication through

The *chars* become new habitats

a method called '*mela shikar*' in this region whereby they are captured by lassoing them from atop a trained female elephant, known as *kunki*. However, in recent times, with the elephant being included in Schedule 1 under the Wildlife Protection Act, this method of trapping elephants has ceased to be.

There is a charming folk tale in Goalpara about why a female always leads an elephant herd. As the story goes, long ago a poor but happy couple Joynath and Joymala lived on the edge of a forest. Joymala generously shared whatever food they could garner with the birds and animals of the forest. The animals too brought fruits and greens for her. But the good days were soon to be over. On one of his visits to the outside world, handsome Joynath was ensnared by a rich widow to make him marry her daughter with promises of a rich dowry that would take care of his first wife too. On returning to the forest, his new wife ill-treated Joymala, banished her to a mud cottage and made her bring water from the river every day. Poor Joymala cried copiously and her tears made the river water salty.

In another part of the forest lived the king of elephants. On finding the river water salty he came to investigate the cause. Moved by Joymala's plight, he proposed marriage to her. But how could a human marry an elephant? So Joymala refused. Meanwhile the sympathetic river rose up and swept away Joynath and his new wife as well as their house. So the elephant king placed homeless Joymala on his back and took her deep into the forest near a waterfall. He poured seven pitchers of water over her head and Joymala turned into a beautiful female elephant. The king elephant married her and taking her as his queen said that every herd from then on would be led by a female.

While it is a charming folk tale, as in other such instances, there is also a grain of truth in it about how nature and man lived harmoniously in the days of yore.

Between western Assam and north Bengal lies a traditional elephant corridor through which wild elephants have been freely moving through centuries in search of food. Today human habitation on this age-old route has disrupted the process, resulting in the increase of man-animal conflicts.

Between western Assam and north Bengal lies a traditional elephant corridor through which wild elephants have been freely moving through centuries ...

In older days, elephants were widely used, and still are to some extent, for transportation, carrying weights, clearing jungles, etc., in the North East. In fact, the discovery of oil at Digboi in upper Assam, reputed to be the oldest working refinery in the world, has something to do with elephants too. British army officers, like Lt. R. Wilcox, had come across evidence of oil and gas in the area. Even Robert Bruce had reported witnessing oil seepage but no exploration was carried out. In 1882, the Assam Railway and Trading Company was laying railway tracks between Dibrugarh and Margherita (so named by an Italian engineer after Queen Margherita) when they found elephants used for clearing jungles showing telltale signs of oil on their feet. Curious, they explored the area. And were they lucky! The name Digboi is supposed to have come from the Canadian engineer W.L. Lake's instructions to the workers, 'Dig boy! Dig!' In 1889 the first commercially viable drilling well was dug and the Assam Oil Company was formed to take over the oil exploration in the country.

Catching wild elephants is quite a risky job. It also means absence from home for long stretches of time. This has led to different types of songs, *maut* (mahout) songs full of pathos:

Right: Near Dhubri the Brahmaputra is a congregation point for boats.

The legendary Netai Dhubuni ghat in Dhubri

Balu til til pankhi kande
Balute paria
Gouriparia maut kande o' sakhi
Ghar bari charia
Aiko charilong Baiko charilong
Charilong sonar puri
Biya koria chariya ashilung o' sakhi
Alpo boyesher nari (Datta, Sarma and Das 1994, 70)

(The sandpiper cries lying in the sand
The *maut* from Gauripur cries, O dear

Cut off from his hearth and home
I left my mother; I left my golden home,
I married and left behind, O dear
A tender-aged bride [O dear]!)

And the woman who is left behind sings:

Pakhi O', mor rajar mahout re
Jedin mahout uzan jai
narir mon mor juria roi re ...

(O my little bird, my mahout rides the king's elephant
The day my mahout goes upstream
I cry silently, o my bird ...)

The name Digboi
is supposed to
have come from
the Canadian
engineer
W.L. Lake's
instructions to
the workers,
'Dig boy! Dig!'

The man sometimes feels helpless too in the jungle:

Bonore haatiko bolab parishu
Habite katilu lata
Shahuror jiyekak bolabo pora nai
dei puri more deha

(I've tamed wild elephants
I've chopped snakes in the jungle
But I can't tame her, this father-in-law's daughter
That's why I'm burning all over)

Then there are also lullaby songs addressed to the captured elephants which are supposed to calm them:

Khera rohona beta, khera rohona
Tor pithit ji howdah kosim
tore gahana beta
khera rohona

(Stand still my dear
I'll place the howdah on your back
It's your jewel
Stand still.)

The profession of elephant-catching was also egalitarian and the men engaged in it were from different castes and creeds but rose above religious divides. In fact, one of the commonest chants while going into the deep jungle runs like this:

Allah, Allah, bolo re bhai
Hai Allah rasul

... there are also lullaby songs addressed to the captured elephants which are supposed to calm them

(Allah, Allah, chant his name, brother
Hai Allah Rasul)

The Goalpara region has a character which distinguishes itself from other parts of the Brahmaputra valley. Living in close proximity with Bengal the culture as well as the language shows the influences of both.

Thus the *Bhawaiya* and *Chatka* songs share a common heritage with north Bengal. The songs do not have any religious overtone and are basically peasant songs enjoyed by both Hindus and Muslims. Sung with the two-stringed *dotara*, the *Bhawaiya* is more serious and plaintive, while the *Chatkas* are funny and lighter and rooted in earthy overtones with emphasis on physical love.

The Goalpara region has a character which distinguishes itself from other parts of the Brahmaputra valley

Chilarai's valour is still remembered

The Panch Pir dargah by the riverbank

Near Dhubri, the Brahmaputra abruptly turns south and enters Bangladesh. Even from the days of the Ahoms the Brahmaputra here was a congregation point of boats engaged in trade. Things not easily available in Assam, like salt, were brought from Bengal and handicrafts, lac, *agar*—a perfume obtained from the local *agar* tree—passed through the river junction. During colonial times too, being at the crossroad of steamer traffic connecting Calcutta and Dhaka and as an entry point to the North East, the town played an important role. In 1883 it was made the headquarter of the Assam Mail Service which established a daily 'single-handed' service between Dhubri and Dibrugarh served by a fleet of fast river steamers built in London and Glasgow and named after different tribes of the North East, such as Naga, Garo, Lushai, Duffla, etc.

Taking advantage of railway connectivity, from 1905 peasants from erstwhile East Bengal started coming to Assam's fertile terrains from the districts of Mymensingh, Pabna, Rangpur, Rajshahi, etc. Though they were initially 'farm settlers' on the sandbank in the riverine area, soon they spread to other parts of the valley. Hard working and enterprising, they have changed the agricultural profile of the valley. They also introduced jute cultivation in Assam.

Dhubri's name is associated with Netai *dhubuni*, the celestial washerwoman who figures in the legend of Beula-Lakhinder and Chand *saudagar*, a rich merchant and a Siva worshipper, from the Sonitpur district on the north bank of the Brahmaputra, as told in *Padma Purana*. According to the story, Manasa, the serpent goddess, was offended by Chand's arrogance and his insults and cursed him by saying that he would lose all his merchandise and that not a single progeny of his would survive the wedding night unless he offered puja to her. The merchant lost his six sons one after another to snakebites but still refused to obey her. He challenged her that his youngest son,

Lakhinder, would survive and he built a house without a single window or opening for the wedding night of Lakhinder and Beula. But even then a tiny hole was made by the builder with the connivance of the goddess while the house was getting constructed. On the wedding night, Manasa 'transformed into a hair-like proportion', entered the house and bit Lakhinder. His wife Beula refused to accept this and took his dead body in a *bhoor* to reach Indrapuri, the abode of the gods, to appeal for reviving him. It was on this journey by the Brahmaputra that she saw Netai *dhubuni* washing clothes on a slab of stone in the midst of the river, which was very unusual. Beula saw that when her little son disturbed her she put him in a comatose spell and then again revived him when the work was over. That convinced Beula that she was no ordinary washerwoman and asked for her guidance to reach Indrapuri. She guided Beula and ultimately Beula managed to obtain the blessing of the *devas* or gods with her exemplary devotion and Lakhinder was given back his life.

Chand *saudagar* agreed to recognise Manasa and offer puja to her, albeit reluctantly. Consequently his other sons were revived and he also got back his lost merchandise.

Suknani Oja or *Maroi Goa Oja*, a branch of the old Oja-Pali performing art of Assam with dance, dialogue and story-telling from Mangaldoi region on the north bank, has as its theme the ballad of Beula-Lakhinder. These ballads and beliefs point to an ancient tradition of snake-worship in Assam, one of the most snake-infested regions in India and a seat of Saivism. Lord Siva always wears a garland of snakes. In Bengal too Manasa puja is common even today.

The legend of Netai *dhubuni* has survived to this day in Dhubri. When you are by the riverside, a meeting point of the tributary Gadadhar and the Brahmaputra, local people point out a huge stone slab still visible in the river claiming it to be that famous washerwoman's stone. They also claim that the stone never gets submerged even when the water level rises a great deal.

Guru Teg Bahadur gurudwara glows in the evening light

Guru Teg Bahadur gurudwara or Dam Dama Sahib ... was built to commemorate the visit of Guru Nanak, the founder of Sikhism

Though the name Dhubri is firmly ensconced in the Netai *dhubuni* legend, in another version, the name is of Bodo origin and comes from the word *dubra*, a variety of grass.

The river bank at Dhubri is serene and beautiful and interspersed with fishing boats and boats for carrying people to the *chars*, some of which have now become permanent habitats of migrants from Bangladesh. Keeping vigil on this last post of a town is a statue of Chilarai, younger brother of Naranarayan, riding a horse, his sword pointing to the sky as if warning the invaders to stay away.

Nearby is the Panch Pir dargah, a *mazar sharif* dedicated to five Sufi saints who had accompanied Ram Singh during his invasion of Assam. People of all religions visit the shrine to offer prayers here.

Dhubri also has the holy Guru Teg Bahadur gurudwara or Dam Dama Sahib. It was built to commemorate the visit of Guru Nanak, the founder of Sikhism. He had come to Assam in 1505 and even met Sri Sankardeva, who was greatly respected by

The river near Dhubri:
ready to leave Assam

the Koch kings and was given land to establish a *satra* at Patbausi near Barpeta which was a part of the Koch kingdom. In fact, Sankardeva had spent his last years here when the Ahoms, steeped in Sakta worship, were not very welcoming of Vaishnavites in upper Assam. The Sikh guru and the Vaishnavite guru were said to have discussed at length the wisdom of worshipping in a simple way as against the excesses of Saktaism and Tantriticism taking hold of the eastern region at that time. From here Guru Nanak took the river route to Sadiya and Parasuramkunda to China, according to descriptions of the Guru's journey in Assam.

Later in 1670, Guru Teg Bahadur came with Ram Singh at the request of the general to help find a peaceful end to the conflict with the Ahoms. Though it did not happen and Ram Singh was defeated at the battle of Saraighat, the ninth Guru had his wish fulfilled of visiting the place, Dhubri, where Guru Nanak stayed for some time. He established the gurudwara in Guru Nanak's memory. Today, Dam Dama Sahib is a well-known pilgrimage centre not only for the Sikhs, but also for people of other communities. Every winter, Sikhs from all over the world visit here on pilgrimage.

In the evening as the rain-laden air blew fresh from the Brahmaputra the evening prayer songs from the gurudwara floated in the air. The gurudwara's white marble façade shone, serene and mysterious, in the twilight and there seemed to be magic in the air.

Perhaps it is right that as the great Brahmaputra bids farewell to the land of Pragjyotishpur, Kamarupa, Assam, on its journey to the sea, this magic is felt once again at a place where the shrines of different communities sit next to each other harmoniously. In older scriptures Assam was often referred to as a land of magic and witchcraft. It was said that outsiders who came to this land would never return as they were captured by a web of mesmerising mantras. This magic was not man-made but of the pristine beauty of the verdant land; the great Brahmaputra and its tributaries making the alluvial soil so fertile that hardly any labour was needed to grow food. A land where nature invoked beautiful patterns on the clothes, where dancing and singing flowed spontaneously under fewer social restraints. No wonder then that those who came here—Kiratas, Aryans, Muslims, Sikhs—chose to stay back in this exquisitely beautiful land.

That is the magic of the Brahmaputra valley, casting a spell on the people to induce them to make it their home and merge in the cauldron of many cultures, many influences. ●

Acknowledgements

While conceptualising the book and later writing it, a number of individuals and institutions helped me tremendously.

I am indebted to eminent folklorist Birendranath Datta for generously sharing his vast knowledge of the folk traditions of Assam.

I am grateful to Nirmal Kanti Bhattacharjee, former editor of Sahitya Akademi's journal, *Indian Literature*, for encouraging me to take forward my idea when I used him as a sounding board.

I am thankful for being able to use an uncompiled song courtesy of Rudra Barua.

I would also like to thank the staff of the Reference Section, Directorate of Library Services, Guwahati, and the National Library, Kolkata, for going an extra mile to facilitate my work.

Officials at the Kaziranga National Park were also very helpful and I acknowledge their help with gratitude.

My colleague Pitamber Newar helped with some of the photographs in the book and I am extremely grateful.

Logistical support was extended by many near and dear ones. I particularly thank H.N. Das, Bonita Das, Minati Das, Rumjhum Borooah, Ruplekha Borah for their help during my travels in Assam.

Last but not the least, I am grateful to my family, husband Arup, children Rimli and Rahul, who have always stood by me and stoically borne my long absences from home.

References

Acharya, Pradip. 1993. *Where Seas Meet.* Guwahati: Lawyer's Book Stall.

——. 2009. Fly-leaf in *Assam-Land & People* published on the 25th anniversary of K.C. Das Commerce College.

Agarwala, Jyoti. 2004. *Jyoti Rachanavali.* Assam: Publication Board.

Ahmed, Kamaluddin. 1994. *The Art and Architecture of Assam.* Guwahati: Spectrum Publications.

Baldizzone, Tiziana and Gianni. 2000. *Tales from the River Brahmaputra: Tsangpo, Brahmaputra, Jamuna.* New Delhi: Timeless Books.

Banikanta Kakati. 1948. *The Mother Goddess Kamakhya.* Guwahati: Punya P. Duara for The Assam Publishing Corporation.

Bareh, Hamlet. 1967. *The History and Culture of the Khasi People.* Guwahati: Spectrum Publications.

Barman, Sivanath. 1982. *Lok-kristir Utsha.* Guwahati: Publication Board.

Barua, Birinchi Kumar. 1964. *History of Assamese Literature.* New Delhi: Sahitya Akademi.

——. 1969. *A Cultural History of Assam.* Guwahati: Lawyer's Book Stall.

Barua, Hem. 1954. *The Red River and the Blue Hills.* Guwahati: Lawyer's Book Stall.

Barua, Kanaklal. 1966. *Early History of Kamarupa.* Guwahati: Lawyer's Book Stall.

Bhattacharyya, Birendra Kumar. 1994. Evolving Culture of the North East. *The Sentinel*, December 31, Guwahati.

Bhuyan, Suryya Kumar. 1947. *Lachit Barphukan and His Times.* Gauhati: Government of Assam, Department of Historical and Antiquarian Studies.

——. 1965. *Studies in the History of Assam.* New Delhi: Omsons Publication.

Biswas, Ranjita. 2012. *As the River Flows HarperCollins Book of Assamese Stories.* India: Harper Perennial.

Borboruah, Hiteswar. 2008. *Ahomar Din.* Guwahati: Publication Board.

Bordoloi, Nirmal Prova. 1986. *Devi.* Guwahati: Sahitya Prakash.

Butler, John. 1855. *Travels and Adventures in the Province of Assam*. Bombay: Smith, Taylor and Co.

Chaliha, Parag. 2008. Assam through the Ages. In *Cultural Heritage of Assam*. Assam: Directorate of Information & Public Relations.

Das, Jugal. 1988. *Gohona-Gathori*. Guwahati: Publication Board.

Datta, B.N. 1980. The Assamese Folk Mind. In *Assam and the Assamese Mind*. Jorhat: Asam Sahitya Sabha.

Datta, B.N., N.C. Sarma and P.C. Das. 1994. *A Handbook of Folklore Material of North-East India*. Guwahati: Anundoram Borooah Institute of Language, Art and Culture.

Doley, Durgeswar. 1980. Assamese Liberalism. In *Assam and the Assamese Mind*. Guwahati: Assam Sahitya Sabha.

Dutta, Arup Kumar. 2001. *The Brahmaputra*. New Delhi: National Book Trust.

Dutta, Debabrata. 1989. *History of Assam*. Calcutta: Sribhumi Publishing Company.

Dutta, Dilip Kumar. 1981. *Bhupen Hazarikar Git Aru Jiban Rath*. Guwahati: Messrs Banalata.

Gait, A. Edward. 1933. *A History of Assam*. Calcutta: Thacker Spink & Co Pvt. Ltd.

Gogoi, Lila. 1982. *Asamor Sanskriti*. Dibrugarh University, Jorhat: Bharati Prakasan.

Goswami, K.D. 1999. Sankardeva: The Innovator and the Composer. Paper presented at National seminar on Sankardeva by Sahitya Akademi, Calcutta.

Goswami, Praphulladutta. 1988. *Bohag Bihu of Assam and Bihu Songs*. Guwahati: Publication Board.

——. 2008. Assam in India's Cultural Stage. In *Cultural Heritage of Assam*. Assam: Directorate of Information & Public Relations.

Krishnan, Ananth. 2011. China maps Brahmaputra, Indus. In *The Hindu*, August 23.

Mahanta, Nirupoma. 2008. Sattras of Assam. In *Cultural Heritage of Assam*. Assam: Directorate of Information & Public Relations.

Nath, D. 2009. *The Majuli Island: Society, Economy & Culture*. New Delhi: Anshah Publication House for Maulana Abul Kalam Azad Institute of Asian Studies.

Nath, Raj Mohan. 1948. *The Background of Assamese Culture*. Guwahati: Dutta Baruah & Co.

Neog, Maheswar. 1983. Introduction to *The Orunodoi (1846-1854)*. Assam: Publication Board.

Phukan, Papori. 2008. The Tai Ahoms of Assam. In *Cultural Heritage of Assam*. Assam: Directorate of Information & Public Relations.

Phukon, Girin. 2009. 'Tais of Northeast India and their Cultural Linkage with Southeast Asia' Institute of Tai Studies & Research, Assam. Lecture delivered at the Institute of Language and Culture for Rural Development, Mahidol University, August 4, in Thailand.

Saikia, Nagen. 1980. *Assam and the Assamese Mind*. Jorhat: Asam Sahitya Sabha

Sarma, Jogendra Nath. 1993. *Asamar Nad-Nadi*. Guwahati: Assam Sahitya Sabha.

See: http://www.plantexplorers.com/explorers/biographies/kingdon-ward/frank-kingdon-ward.htm.

Sharma, Jayeeta, Daniel J. Walkowitz and Barbara Weinstein. 2011. *Empire Garden: Assam and the Making of India*. Duke University Press.

Shastri, Ajay Mitra. 2002. Tribalism and Aryanisation. In *'Ancient North East India: Pragjyotishpur' Lecture Series North East University, Shillong*. New Delhi: Aryan Books International.

Vasudev, Aruna. 2008. Editor's Note to *P.C. Barua* by Shoma A. Chatterji, vii. New Delhi: Wisdom Tree.

Index